creating
heaven
on earth

Robert Lester Peck

Personal Development Center
Lebanon, CT 2001

www.personaldevcenter.com

2 3 4 5 6 7 8 9 10

—Publisher's Note—

This second printing, October 2021, of the original 2001 publication of *Creating Heaven on Earth* contains minor editorial corrections throughout the text, format improvements, a reformat of the "Glossary of Important Terms" section, and a correction of the title "The Emerald *Table*" to "The Emerald *Tablet*."

Translation of Greek terms and Sanskrit terms (with Harvard/Kyoto respellings) of the *Paratrimshika* (Thirty Verses), *The Sermon on the Mount*, *The Emerald Tablet*, and *The Gospel of Thomas* are by Robert Lester Peck unless otherwise noted in the text.

Cover design by: Lois Rivard.

Personal Development Center
P.O. Box 93
South Windham, Connecticut 06266

ISBN 13: 978-0917828-09-6 (Paperback)
ISBN 10: 0-917828-09-7 (Paperback)

Printed in the United States of America

Table of Contents

Preface ~ What is Heaven on Earth?

Heaven on earth is that exuberant and joyful state of mind and body that allows you to find and make manifest your deepest yearnings or what you truly seek in life. This state of mind converts the mundane into the transformational and changes daily drudgery into exciting challenges. Heaven on earth opens and leads to your life-long dreams.

Society and its institutions, however, have long suppressed the access to heaven in order to keep individuals bound and conforming to their control. This suppression is simply done by obscuring and hiding the awareness and access to the lower heart and the five separate elements that constitute heaven.

The liberating elements of Heaven on earth, described in all of the original major religious writings of the world, are:

Oneness: At oneness with both your inner and outer worlds, non-judgmental or able to see, accept and fully interact with the world as it really is;

Quickened: Able to find your own inner creative and vitalizing energy to continuously change and transform your self and world;

Ecstatic: Joyful, radiant and free of your own restraints to fully respond emotionally;

i

Voluptuous: Sensual and responsive to self and others to fully physically experience life; and

Changeable: Able to take on any desired new identity and existence to fully live your life.

This book describes the elements and their powers in very practical as well as historical and scientific terms, and most importantly tells of how they can be found and used to add the vault of heaven and its powers to your present world and life.

1. Introduction

Heaven on earth is not just a myth or religious concept, but rather is associated with an exalted, creative and ecstatic state of mind and body. This Heaven is not something that existed only in some distant past, but has been experienced by many people through the ages on into the modern world. This exalted state can be described as being built upon five basic elements or characteristics that are individually experienced by almost everyone, yet are also hidden under false descriptions from a society that discourages adults from experiencing them.

The acceptance of the idea of a Heaven on earth may be made easier with the realization that there is a self-created Hell on earth. The existence of this Hell is, surprisingly, generally accepted in society even though it is not commonly discussed. Hell on earth, like Heaven on earth, can be described with five separate elements using words that are well known and accepted. The five elements of Heaven and Hell can also be perceived to be variants of five elements that describe the normal Social world as listed in the following table:

Hell	*Social*	*Heaven*
Enervated	Energized	Quickened

Isolated	Responsive	Oneness
Critical	Accepting	Ecstatic
Unfeeling	Caring	Voluptuous
Nobody	My Self	New Person

Perhaps the majority of readers will identify themselves as shifting often from a *Social* element to the corresponding element of *Hell* and less frequently shifting to the right towards *Heaven*. In thinking of the elements that describe Heaven, you will probably start to feel concern, fear or an aversion to what the words suggest. The aversion results primarily from the shifting of the actual meaning of the words over many centuries. This shift in the original meanings has given the elements very negative characteristics in today's materialistic world. However, the original meanings of the words were quite positive.

As an introduction to the accurate descriptions of the meanings of the words of the elements of Heaven, first consider the world of *first love*. Most individuals would probably list their first love as being the closest example of what they might have called Heaven on earth and generally can remember quite vividly their inner feelings as well as their frustrations. A generalized listing of the various inner feelings and changes that occur during first love are:

1. Intense vitality or quickening,[1]
2. Union and oneness,
3. A high or craziness,
4. The thrill of physical sensual contact, and
5. The power of becoming a new person.

Every single one of these characteristics, however, is considered to be in conflict with modern society which requires everyone to be conforming and integrated into its whole. Families, employers, religions, and groups, in general, do not long tolerate any individual with the above characteristics or elements of first love.

Children, however, experience some of the elements of Heaven in their imaginative games. Adults quietly experience them during intense joy and success. Some of the elements are also found when individuals become lost in sharing ideas and experiences with others. Heaven on earth is approached during creative moments, when the world appears to open and yields up its resources; or more commonly, in the moments of threat or demands when an inner strength, will, and knowledge suddenly rise within you to meet the challenge.

---

[1] See *Quicken* in Glossary.

This book looks closely at the characteristics of evolving and joyfully creative individuals and their Heavens and describes how these characteristics can be refound and used to build your own Heaven on earth.

2. The Pieces of Heaven on Earth

C hapter One mentioned some of the experiences found in first love that serve as an excellent introduction into what constitutes the characteristics of Heaven on earth. First love can be described as:

1. finding a state of being highly animated or quickened in all that you do,

2. being in a state of union or oneness with the loved one,

3. possessing a high similar to some drug state as you lose your mental constraints and go crazy with joy,

4. being overpowered by the mere presence of the loved one and the intense pleasure of contact and touch, and

5. becoming a new person facing a brand-new future.

Similarly, children at play can be observed to have the same five characteristics and hence have become models for religious teachings. Consider for example, how a child becomes completely lost in an imaginary game with others where the animation and intense joy is quite obvious. A child radiates the role that is being played to such an extent that the child fully becomes the king, witch, or other role required in the game. The game may require suffering, anger, love, solicitude, etc., which children readily find. Many times children require an outside force such as a parent to return them back to their normal conditioned role.

It is not just children and lovers, however, who experience pieces of Heaven. Almost everyone has had those experiences of losing yourself, being carried away, or experiencing extreme joy without the normal judgmental process of the conditioned brain. Union is many times experienced in conversations where limitations as to what or how you may speak are lost, and everything that is said becomes perfect and time ceases to exist. There is the recognition of how during these times you become animated with an extra quickening force flowing in your body. Your mental controls likewise drop away and you can go crazy as you get carried away with some new feelings or thoughts. In most of these types of intense openings to others, you draw closer together and touching each other is not uncommon as you use your hands to further reinforce your feelings. When you leave each other, it may take hours before you feel that you have gained your normal composure and self.

Creative individuals also report similar experiences as they fall into their creative spaces. An idea, concept, feeling or vision is obtained that immediately becomes the focal point of the mind. The concept becomes overwhelming in its clarity, beauty or possibility. The mind and body become animated. Thus, the story of Archimedes seems quite reasonable when he jumped out of his bath and ran out into the street shouting, "*Eureka*!" after he had discovered why things float.

There is an intense joy and attraction for the new idea or revelation that becomes an epiphany just as can be found with the view of a glorious sunset that sweeps through the soul.

There are also experiences of Heaven on earth that are easily listed as being religious or spiritual, such as the feelings described in the Twenty-third Psalm of the Bible or the poem *Dark Night of the Soul* by Saint John of the Cross. In these examples the experiencing of Heaven can be related in religious terms as being:

1. At oneness.
2. Quickened or vitalized.
3. Ecstatic, radiant and of another world.
4. Soft, sensitive and responsive or voluptuous.[2]
5. Reborn into being another person.

This book will explain more about these five characteristics of Heaven on earth, but for the moment each element will be briefly introduced.

The term *quickening* has long been used to describe an inner creational or transformational energy. Historically, it is related to the first sensation of life from the fetus which was felt as rapid vibrations and was compared to that of a fish. The relationship to a fish was further supported by the observations that the

---

[2] See *Voluptuous* in Glossary.

early embryos of mammals look like fish. The symbol of a fish, therefore, became the symbol of quickening or the energy behind a higher life form and was incorporated within the Zodiac as well as in early Christianity. The rising energy found in applying the martial arts or the ability to do the unexpected or the normally impossible tasks is called *quickening*. *Quickening* is the rising of energy from the inner power center that makes you more alive.

Oneness is characterized by the loss of egocentricity and the feeling that you are being controlled by an outer or higher world rather than by your own immediate efforts. This state is described as being carried away by the situation or by losing yourself in the discussions, activities or insights. You become at *oneness* or in bondage to the role that you are playing with others who are also in bondage or at *oneness*. This *oneness* is not without guidance as you find knowledge within yourself that seemingly appears without effort. You know the truth of things deep within yourself. Another manner of expressing this is that you step into a world that is under some higher or Divine control.

Ecstasy is experienced as pleasure that keeps increasing. For instance, each moment becomes more and more intense and exciting and your mind becomes filled with the desire and expectation for even more. It is commonly described as going crazy with rising pleasure or joy. *Ecstasy* further feeds the *quickening*, and the rising *quickening* fees the *ecstasy*.

The *voluptuous* nature has the meaning of wanting to be close to others, desirous of sharing as well as enjoying touching or being touched. It is not sexual lust but rather the holistic feeling of the joining and uniting of souls as well as of bodies and a common presence. It is easily compared to the couple in love who cannot keep their hands off of each other. *Voluptuous* nature also is experienced in cuddling or snuggling with another person or object such as a teddy bear. It includes the pleasure of wearing soft clothing or of being enveloped in softness and warmth.

The term *reborn* is taken from religious and psychological expressions meaning becoming a new person in body and mind. It can also be stated as taking on a new role and personality in life, but unlike the old role, there is a complete faith in the future. The new life is obtained without limitations other than those that are self-imposed.

One additional term needs to be clarified and that is the term *Heaven* which normally has so many meanings different from that required in this book. Generally, in the original religious usage, the manner in which the term was applied defined the meaning. For instance, the expressions such as "birds fly in heaven" and "the sun rises in heaven" all speak of heaven as the sky above. Similarly, the creator of the universe lives in the heaven far removed as do the departed souls. This heaven is not accessible from this earth and is generally considered to be out in space somewhere. However, the term *Kingdom of Heaven* (*Kingdom of God*) as used in the New Testament of the Bible as well as in the earlier *Gospel of Thomas* points to a self-created Heaven on earth. Jesus taught that you create this kingdom by using the inner power and that its entrance is in front of you. He gives many parables about this kingdom that are very confusing if they are assumed to be about a heaven above or found only in an after-life. The usage of the word kingdom is synonymous with the palace or court of a king. This kingdom is therefore associated with pleasure, grandeur, and satisfaction of your desires, as well as power. This kingdom is so pleasurable that the teachings tell how you will give up everything so that you may stay there. Jesus can be seen as emphasizing the *oneness* aspect of *Heaven* or the inner guiding power beyond the conscious mind that must be trusted. This *Kingdom of Heaven* is therefore the same as Heaven on earth as will be used in this book.

Other writings in the Bible do not describe a separate Heaven, but rather speak of some of the characteristics of Heaven on earth. The word *righteous* is widely used in both the old and New Testaments of the Bible to describe the state of being in Heaven on earth. A *righteous* person was successful, joyful, clean, just, and driven by being fulfilled, balanced or complete. To these individuals, the Bible promises that they will be given or have the listed characteristics that are associated with being in Heaven on earth. It should be noted that the word *righteous*[3] has the modern meaning of obeying law, but the original meaning was "to fully be." This term *righteous* can be seen to correspond to terms used in other religions such as being enlightened, liberated, freed, or perfected.

The remainder of this book will delve further into the characteristics or the elements associated with Heaven on earth and how they can be used to create your own Heaven on earth.

---

[3] See *Righteous* in Glossary.

3. Quickening

To *quicken* means to make alive or more alive. Quickening can be described as the manifesting of a mystical life force that imparts increased mental, spiritual or physical activity to an object or existing life form. Quickening in humans is evidenced with a departure from the status quo or from conditioned behavior and thinking.

First love is an excellent example of quickening because the increase in life force in both of the lovers is so noticeable. The lovers take on a vitality and an expanded interest in life that is in sharp contrast to their previous existence. They find a special energy to do things that they would not have even considered doing before, such as staying up all night talking or pursuing some common challenging goal. Their physical and mental health improves markedly, and they both take on a radiance that is well-recognized. This special energy or quickening is not associated with lust or the simple satisfying of physical desires, but rather that which is used to fully meet each moment together so as to not waste one second. Young lovers have the quickening to constantly reach into the oncoming moment to further enrich each moment of life together. They become more and more alive by feeding and being nourished by each other.

Despite their odd behavior, the lovers are actually more acceptable to the social world in that they can be more efficient and cheerful in their daily tasks and interactions with others. It is evident that their world is changed in that many of the males become more loquacious and perhaps boring to their friends as their conversations seem to want to center on their love, but they are seen as more awakened and alive nonetheless. Some of the females likewise can find the absence from their lovers depressing, yet first love seems to be as a stimulant to most lovers who become more alert and alive to their existence. They certainly demonstrate an opening to the world with an increased quickening to fully meet the immediate demands of the world.

One surprising aspect of the energy of first love for virgins is that it is seldom perceived as leading initially to sexual intercourse. Their energies are placed into exploring their mutual worlds as a stage of pre-bonding rather than into enflaming biological urges. Touching, getting close and the exploring of each other's body and reactions are, of course, exciting and rewarding; however, it is not done for possession or control, but for sharing, uniting and giving. This desire to share and give requires quickening in order to increase both the sensitivity to each other as well as a heightened response back to each other. Quickening stimulates both the sense organs as well as oneness.

This quickening of lovers is also similar to the quickening found by individuals who dedicate themselves to some form of improvement of their lives as will be discussed later.

There is another type of quickening that is quite spectacular because of its suddenness and power that can instantly change an individual. The Bible uses the term *astonied*[4] (thunderstruck) to indicate this state of being overpowered with quickening that leads to the attainment of a revelation or insight. Being astonied can be compared with the experiences described by the Eastern Sanskrit term *vajra* which means a thunderbolt that can transform an individual. Religious writings tend to credit the sudden rise in quickening to the sudden influence of a spirit, God, power or of an inner rising force. The supernatural deed of an individual to save someone's life or the sudden insight that changes the immediate or future world can be explained by this sudden increase in quickening.[5]

Many individuals have found the sudden quickening in facing an imminent danger or excitement such as their automobile spinning out of control or the sudden awareness of an answer to a long-term problem that must now be solved. The increasing of quickening is many times described as the experiencing of a rising excitement, heat, vibration, electricity, tensioning, or warmth from the sexual region. This feeling is generally quite pleasurable and can stun you. During these moments of quickening, there is often no fear or other emotion, time slows or stands still and you have increased mental capabilities that seem to open your mind to another source of information

---

[4] See *Astonied* in Glossary.
[5] Peck (1999), Ch. 4

This form of quickening must be the result of a combination of complex hormonal release as well as a unique mental process that directs the sensors and responses of the body to meet some sudden arising or intense demand. For instance, the release of adrenaline, which is probably one of the hormones contributing to quickening, stimulates the muscles such that they can meet special demands. However, it also increases the sense organs to better detect the outer world and increases the acuity of the brain to more fully understand and relate to the outer world.

One very important consideration of the rising of the quickening is that it is not obtained by direct conscious effort. This can be compared with your inability to control the secretion of hormones following some emotional experience. Quickening is generally only found with surrendering to an outside power or situation or in searching for some knowledge. Religious and success stories abound with individuals who find quickening to change their worlds.

The nearly universal description of the source of quickening is that it starts deep within your body. It seems somehow to come from your very center of being and has a power over your entire body and mind. The word *heart*[6] was used to describe its location that had the meaning of being the very center of something. Your heart was therefore the center of your being and

---

[6] See *Heart, hrit, hridaya* in Glossary.

contained the source of quickening and was universally described as residing in the lower abdomen, belly or sexual region by the majority of the early religious writings.[7] The Jewish writings used the Hebrew words *leb* and *meah* to refer to the heart that was located within the intestines, belly, or bowels.

Within this *lower heart* the spirit of the individual was assumed to dwell whose mystical powers were believed to be stimulated with the deep breathing experienced during the overcoming of life's obstacles and challenges. The correspondence of breath and spirit was so strong that the word for *spirit* in ancient Greek and Hebrew texts was "deep exhalation" (*pneuma* in Greek and *ruwach* in Hebrew). This explains the importance of the use of the strong exhalation of the breath in early religious rituals as well as its usage in martial arts. In contrast, the *soul* was identified with the word for "light breathing" (*psuche* in Greek and *nephesh* in Hebrew) and was associated with the animal sentient principle located in the chest.

The location of the heart was later changed to the chest where it became identified with the blood-pumping organ. This may have been due in part to the old usage of the Greek word *kardia* that meant "an organ with two orifices" and hence could be either the stomach or the upper pumping organ. The shift in location can also be briefly explained with the Christian belief in the

---

[7] Chapter 9

blood atonement of Jesus as the sacrificial Lamb of God, which replaced the earlier Jewish blood rituals using animal sacrifice. The Sacred Heart of the risen Jesus, as the source of the redeeming blood, became the center for the inspiration and power source for believers. This belief in the power of blood then became the reason for the change of inner power from the lower abdomen to the chest. To further increase the importance of blood and pumping heart, worshippers also engaged in the ritual of drinking the sacred blood of Jesus that would further unite their blood, body and purpose with that of Jesus.

With the shifting of what was believed to be the individual's center of being up into the chest and its pumping heart, some of the old religious disciplines no longer were understandable. The disciplines that applied pressure to the perineum or lower sexual area, for instance, were no longer considered to be of value. One such discipline was the simple act of sitting that was advocated worldwide. This practice can be seen as activating the lower heart, and hence quickening.

There are two entirely different physical methods of sitting. One fits the modern concept of being comfortable and relaxed, generally with the back supported and reclined to some degree, and with a soft pad under the buttocks and perineum. The other method, used for stimulation or increasing the quickening rather than relaxation, has the back unsupported and upright, tummy relaxed and protruding, and the perineum in contact with the support of the seat. Much of the world also sits cross-legged which has the advantage of stretching and providing more pressure on the perineum that is able, in turn, to apply direct pressure and stimulation to the lower center.

The perineum is one of the sensitive areas of the body that a child loves to stimulate or have stimulated. Adults learn to let a child sit on the knee or foot and then bounce the child up and down with obvious enjoyment from the child. Children, in playing, love to fall or bounce on their buttocks or apply direct pressure to the perineum with such activities as straddling and then sliding along a tree limb or bars on the playground. The older children learn how to bounce on a teeter-totter or how to enjoy sledding down a bumpy slope which also stimulates the perineum and inner center.

Pressure or pounding on the perineum puts pressure on or massages the inner lower glands as well as changes the pressure within the spinal fluid. The sacred bone, or the sacrum, has holes along its length that may couple the pressure arising from the perineum to the fluid within the spine. The change in pressure of the lower spinal fluid is then transmitted upwards to the base of the brain thereby also providing some stimulation to the glands in the head.

Rocking on the perineum is known to change the body and mind. As for instance, a wonderful therapy for autistic or severely depressed children is obtained with bareback riding on a horse, which results in the direct massaging of the perineum. Simple sitting and rocking are also found therapeutic to both children and adults who may find relief in emotional problems such as grief or apprehension.

Even greater stimulation can be obtained for the lower center or lower heart with inner movement of the lower abdominal muscles. Examples of this motion is found with crying or laughing, both of which are known to change the mind, body and view of the outer world. Deep exhalations, with the lungs emptied, press on the lower abdomen with surprising results. One interesting example of the change in breathing is found when you become demanding or authoritative. You breathe out forcibly using a lower lung capacity rather than the filled lungs. Using the downward deep exhalation changes your voice such that others react to it, giving you more attention and respect. This deep exhalation is fundamental to mastering the martial arts as well as loosening the source of quickening.

You may have noticed that when you are startled, you make a sudden gasp of exhalation or inhalation which stimulates the lower abdominal breathing muscles to ready or quicken the body to meet an emergency. If you wish to increase your inner energy, exhale strongly and let your lungs fill (without forced inhalation) to half capacity and repeat. You have, however, been taught the reverse of taking a deep breath and then breathing out slowly without effort. (Children must be conditioned to breathe this way to make them easier to control and able to learn.)

The value of quickening is illustrated in a story about the origin of the martial arts when a group of yogis in ancient India were suddenly set upon by bandits. The yogis, who had mastered the breath and churning of the abdomen, found that they could easily vanquish the bandits because they could move faster as well as anticipate the moves of the bandits. In order to verify this power of quickening, a group of middle-aged adults with increased quickening were measured as they clapped their hands in response to a sound.[8] Their speed of response was then compared to a group of 12-13-year-old children as well as a middle-aged control group of adults. The results are quite surprising and do support the ancient story as well as modern claims of increased reaction times in emergencies. The children responded on the average 30% faster than the adult control group, as normally expected; however, the quickened group responded 27% faster than the young children with a man of nearly 70 years beating the time of the fastest child.

Some Chinese martial art systems[9] list the lower abdomen as the source of *chi* or quickening and teach that this lower center must be stimulated with various breathing exercises and motions of the body. The early Indian systems[10] were more descriptive of the lower center (*svadishthana*, "place of standing of the self") and even the West used the term of *solar plexus* ("place

---

[8] Peck (1998), Appendix
[9] Lu K'uan (1973)
[10] Peck (1976) and Woodroffe (1974)

of connections to the sun") in a similar manner. (This term is understandable if the usage of the word sun is recognized as the center for interacting with the outer world.[11])

The ancient system of alchemy was developed, in part, to convert the latent bioenergy of the body into a higher form of energy. The alchemical process began in the lower chambers of the athanor (body) with heat and mixing in the presence of a special catalyst (the stone of the philosopher) and is many times depicted in sexual terms and symbolic scenes such as the nude embrace of a prepubescent boy and girl, the union of God and Goddess, or the union of the sun and moon.[12]

There is an optimum standing posture for supporting quickening as well as a posture that suppresses quickening. Modern society teaches and supports the latter which has the tummy and buttocks pulled in, making the lower body become straight, tight, and flat. You are taught, starting in elementary school, that you look fit and healthy with this posture. Quickening, however, demands a relaxed and expanded lower abdomen such as found in young children with the buttocks and stomach protruding outwards such that the perineum can be stimulated with the pressure from the movement of the thighs. This relaxed posture is also the correct posture for many of the early martial arts.

---

[11] Chapter 9; Peck (1998), Ch. 13-14; Peck (1988), Ch. 17
[12] Ibid.

The early religious writings of many of the major religions taught that sexual intercourse diminishes quickening and hence sex should be used only for procreation. Almost all ancient philosophies assumed that the creative energy of the body is limited and, if used for sexual orgasm or the creation of a new life, will be lost for quickening. To support this concept, consider how you have experienced that your world opens and your senses increase with an extended period of absence from sexual release. You are also very much aware of how your world closes down with reduced vitality after sexual gratification. Modern society and its institutions know that individuals who have frequent sexual intercourse are more easily managed and hence encourage frequent sex. Consider for instance, how society lauds sexual prowess, teaches sexual techniques and contraceptives in public schools, and promotes conjugal prison visits.

The early writings, however, taught the necessity of a special form of union between a male and a female and the merger of their two distinct characteristics that increased quickening. Some of the writings pointed to a higher form of a male/female coupling that because of its extremely ecstatic and transformational power has suffered suppression over the centuries. This coupling was without penetration or orgasm and increased quickening, voluptuousness and ecstasy, but this topic is beyond the scope of this book.[13]

Quickening is often considered to be a feminine or feminizing force, which may explain the sex of the universal great *Quickener*, i.e., *Mother Nature*. The feminine sexual-like feelings encountered within the lower center can many times become very strong with the sense of inner female-like responses.[14] It is this strong feminine inner feeling that, no doubt, led to many religions describing the inner controlling power as an indwelling feminine spirit. It is easy to postulate that the feminine form of religious garb around the world is a result of the feminine feelings arising from quickening.

There is an opposite masculine force associated with quickening that is related to the outer creations or changes that are evidenced coming from a quickened person. The creative and innovative actions are generally described as coming from an inner masculine force. Later the quickening and the driving forces will be described as coming forth from an inner center that contains both. Many religions describe this combined sexual experience as having an androgynous nature and many ancient gods were depicted with both masculine and feminine characteristics.

---

[13] Peck (1998), Ch. 21 see *Maithuna*.
[14] Peck (1998), Ch. 19

The increase of quickening and the resulting opening and sharing with others is first experienced in the imaginary games of childhood during which a child must fully respond to the imaginary characters or roles that everyone puts on. As children are able to fully find the oneness with each other and the necessary energy or quickening to fully play their roles, they step into the magical world of oneness and ecstasy that quickly overpowers all of the players.

This sense of quickening is found many times as an adult where there is no fear of repercussions from your statements or actions or judgment of others. One familiar example of this quickening is experienced during a trip where you find yourself bored and looking for something of interest. Many times, you can easily initiate a conversation with the person next to you and find that both of you quickly get pulled into the resulting discussion. Many times, it seems that you are both of one mind and you become quite quickened as you compare stories or anecdotes. You both become aware of the direction of the discussion and are anxious to assist in its unfolding. The discussion becomes as an exciting game where you both know the rules and the assumed roles that you both play.

During this time together you sense a oneness as time seems to pass ever so quickly or has no meaning. There is only complete acceptance of the other person without any judgment. It is as if you have known and played with each other for much of your lifetimes. That you exhibited quickening during this process is evidenced by you becoming fully awake and alert, whereas initially you felt fatigued, bored and enervated. You have probably also seen the same vitalization in a child who was sitting dejected and doing very little until he is pulled into a game with other children.

Quickening initiates the development of another power within the body that is associated with providing creativity, intuition and what can be called guidance. For instance, many individuals who find quickening in facing an emergency also find an opening of the mind that provides an insight into what they should do. Some individuals find that under some strong demand which quickens them, they can become quite creative. The creative conversation above can be credited in part to this power. Many practices that can be called religious or spiritual can likewise produce a quickened state in which philosophical, scientific or religious questions may be answered.

This creative inner guiding power is called by many names from the Holy Spirit to indwelling gods to *kundalini* by various groups and religions. This book will attempt to avoid the use of such names because of the conditioned interpretation given to them. Instead, the simple name of *inner power* will be used in the following chapters.

4. Oneness

Oneness is characterized as being awake and aware but not being controlled by conscious thoughts or actions. There are no judgements. Oneness is found with others when there is complete trust and the group responds as of one mind. Oneness is having total security and confidence, or the acceptance of being controlled by some higher beneficent power that is a part of you and your immediate world.

Many individuals report that their happiest moments were found during the times when they stepped into some experience that was so overpowering that they lost any concern or control of the future. In oneness, there is the acceptance and trusting in the guidance offered by the enveloping power that replaces individual conscious control. This enveloping and beneficent power is described in the marketplace with many terms such as the power of a game or of camaraderie, a guiding hand, luck, fortune, inspiration, or some form of the Divine. In this book the power will be referred to as the *inner power* to avoid confusion with the interpretations of the other names. The inner power is assumed to have its center within the lower heart, as described by ancient writings, and is the source of experienced oneness with others as will be described in Chapter Nine.

There are two very distinct types of oneness. The most common form of oneness that is experienced by most modern individuals is the oneness found in watching a movie or television. The initial desire is to forget the trials and tribulations of the day and sink into a passive open awareness dominated and controlled by entertainment. While initially relaxing and restorative, this type of oneness can lead to total oblivion as awareness is allowed to diminish with the surrendering of control and judgment. This type of oblivion is very attractive to individuals wishing to escape the frustrations and demands of life, and it is the goal of some religions that describe it as sinking into oneness with the *All* or into the ocean of creation. It is the state of *Nirvana*[15] of the Buddhists. This state of oblivion can be experienced while concentrating upon an object that requires minimal effort to maintain the concentration such as a repeated mental word, candle, icon or repetitive prayer and then essentially letting the non-reactive object absorb any thoughts or feelings.

The second type of oneness is the opposite of the above in that the object concentrated upon is a person, activity or other creative source that then interacts back to such an extent that it controls the mind. You experience this, for instance, when you find yourself in a highly animated conversation with others and the conversation overrides your sense of control. When you submit or surrender to this state of being overpowered, you generally can open to the source of the *inner power*. This opening allows you then to listen and respond to whatever will be said without any bias or expectation.

---

[15] See *Nirvana* in Glossary.

You do not, as in normal conversations, think about what you are going to say or what you think they are going to say. Instead, you find yourself in complete union with what is being said and you respond without any conscious volition. You might, for instance, say later that the conversation overpowered all of you such that all of you became lost in the discussion. This type of oneness is characterized as being fully alive but reaching and working for more. It is this interactive type of union that characterizes Heaven on earth.

Interactive or shared oneness is found in first love with the total merging of mind, body and purpose following the intense yearning for each other. Separation becomes painful and yet the lovers cannot possibly become close enough when they are together. Their immaturity is reflected in this inability to fully become one, and unfortunately, modern society seldom tells them how to increase their union other than to falsely promise that they can find it in sexual coitus.

First love also can be used as an illustration of the steps and methods used in finding a union with someone. There is first an attraction toward the other person. Then there is the concentration on the other person[16] followed by fully seeing the other person without the normal judgments.[17] There is then the beginning of oneness as each seeks to fully understand the other and

---

[16] See *Dharana* in Glossary.
[17] See *Dhyana* in Glossary.

to be fully understood so that they start to interact together without any barriers.[18] Union is then found during their open interactions when it is discovered that, somehow, they react completely together as one mind[19] as if they find some omnipresent mind that controls them both similar to a game controlling children at play. This union can perhaps be better explained by saying that the inner powers of the other person become united with your own and that both individuals therefore respond as one.

This yearning to find interactive oneness can be compared with one of religion's fundamental commandments of loving God and your neighbor with all of your heart, soul and might. This unreserved love, called *agapao*[20] in the early Greek Septuagint Bible (300 BCE) was translated later with a reduced meaning by modern churches to being only the act of giving money or charity. The word *charity* (*agape*) unfortunately has also been altered from its original meaning of "being overpowered and interacting with love" to "the act of giving." Love of God and neighbor is therefore now widely understood as giving money to a church or a charitable institution. The best expression of your love for someone is likewise understood as giving gifts to the other person. The larger the gift, the greater your love. A little thinking can quickly help the reader to understand why social institutions teach the

---

[18] See *Samadhi* in Glossary.

[19] See *Samyama* in Glossary; Peck (1994), Practices pp.70-89.

[20] See *Agapao* in Glossary; Peck (1999), see References.

giving of costly gifts rather than the true meaning of *agapao* or *agape*.

Today few people can understand true *oneness* or what the early religious commandment of loving God with all of your heart, soul and might mean. Even fewer have experienced it. Part of the confusion might be traced to the change from finding oneness with God to appeasing or supplicating God. Similarly, there is a modern change from finding oneness with someone with whom you wish to find union with, to appeasing or supplicating them with gifts. There is also the modern tendency to try to possess or obtain power over those that you desire to find union with.

Our society, for instance, lauds romance that consists of wooing a person, which generally means to solicit or entreat attention from the other person. If the other person agrees to the possible romance, they too become solicitous, and both attempt to become perfect in the eyes of the other person so that they have more to give to the other person. Romance is the giving of what the other person is believed to desire. This giving can be contrasted with the very opposite aspect of first love when each person is already perfect in the eyes of the other as they really are. There can be nothing of value to be given, but rather there is only the sharing of each other's perfection. The romantic wooing can also be compared to the worship within a church wherein the worshippers don their best clothes and give offerings to their god in the expectation of the reception of gifts in return. In general, these relationships continue with expectations of return gifts because of the obligations associated with their giving rather than the expectation of finding oneness.

There is another important yet little discussed aspect of oneness or union that needs to be addressed. This is the uniting of the future with the present. Almost everyone has experienced an introduction to this oneness with what is commonly called a *deja vu* in which the unique moment appears to have already been experienced. Another common case is like buying a magazine for no apparent reason only to find later that it has an article about some project that you have planned to undertake.

Consider the simple example of attempting to remember a name. You, for instance, might be engaged in some conversation and suddenly you wish to bring forth a name of someone that you know. However, your mind cannot recall the name and despite running through the alphabet looking for some connection to the starting letter, your mind remains a blank. Your experience in remembering names may then surface and you then tell the group that the name is not recalled, but that it will come to you later. You then forget about it until a few minutes later in the midst of a sentence, the name suddenly appears and you are then able to bring it forth.

A more complicated example of uniting the future with the present can be experienced when you are looking for an answer such as finding some way to hang a picture in some difficult place on a non-conventional wall. Try as hard as you might, the normal mounting techniques will not work, so you resolve that you will put off worrying about it and instead trust that the next time you go to a hardware store, you will find something that will work. Later, you may be on another errand to the store, when suddenly you find a gadget that will hang your picture, even though you were not consciously thinking of the problem at that time. In this exercise you were not looking for a specific item or name, but something that would fill the need, and when the answer appeared on the scene your previous resolution identified it at some subconscious level.

Consider another case. You have volunteered to assist in putting on an amateur play and have been asked to find costumes. Within your very small budget, you have managed to find costumes for all of the characters except for one. To provide the proper costume for the remaining role, you have the general image of a painted mask, attached wings, special footwear and some ancient-type clothing. You are looking for something in the present that can be altered to somehow fit something in the future. You therefore find yourself wandering into a store having a final sellout of store fixtures and later your friend's attic, where you unexpectedly discover the perfect costume pieces. You know that you are successful when the cast is thrilled with your costumes and the play becomes a success. You have lived up to your reputation of being creative and getting a job done.

Even though the above examples of uniting the future with the present may appear simple and straightforward to you, many cannot understand the hidden source of the answers as arising from an *inner power.* Many people for instance, will go to their pocket listing of names and phone numbers, go to a clerk in the store, or find a costume supply house for their answers. They may well pride themselves upon their efficiency and organization and look askance at any attempt by you to explain that the answers just come to you, provided of course, that you don't think about it.

There is another popular experience of feeling that you should do something or that God told you to do something. This experience is almost always the result of conditioned brain activity that results in further brain analysis before you take any action. The state of oneness can be differentiated from this state by a simple fact that in oneness you are already doing something and there is no time for a choice or analysis. For instance, if you have to think about whether you should buy something, it is not from an *inner power* gained from oneness, but a product of your conscious mind.

There is another differentiation that is required and that is between what you want or desire to do and what you are dedicated to do. Wanting and desiring are almost always the result of societal conditioning and are identifiable by the pressure to be important or pleased. The result of a dedication is seldom experienced by thoughts in the moment, but rather by what you are already doing and where your life is going. If you do not have a deep dedication in life then you are driven by your conditioned wants and desires.

Some individuals are able to set a course toward some remote goal in life and then, to the amazement of those around them manage to reach their goal despite severe oppositions. For instance, the stories of children born with disabilities who then resolve to overcome their limitations and finally reach their goals are legendary. Likewise, stories of individuals learning new skills to obtain better jobs despite hardships are common, as are the stories of successful entrepreneurs who started with only a dream of what they wanted to find.

Friedrich Nietzsche, a critical German philosopher, states that your destiny controls the immediate moment in your life after the breaking of the bondage to your present life.[21] This requires the uniting of your present activities with your future goal or to your dedicated destination in life and then breaking free of all of those conditioned responses that keep you from reaching your own destiny.

There are, however, a few individuals who are able to break their bonds to their conditioned lives and trust that they will with time and effort find the world of their dreams. Those individuals that do manage to break their bonds and seek with vigor their destiny will

---

[21] Nietzsche (1954), Preface, Aphorisms 3-7

generally describe unexpected occurrences that opened new doors to them. The unexpected happenings resulted from being in oneness with their world such that they were able to react to the sudden prompting or impulses that were outside of their normal responses as was previously described.

Another experience of oneness with the future is found when you find yourself in a creative frame of mind. It might start, for instance, after you have contemplated some difficult problem without any results. You may have pushed the problem aside in your mind but much later, you suddenly see an answer all at once, even to the fine details as it would appear in the future. It is as if you suddenly stepped into the future world where the answer to the problem was manifested and you are simply observing it. As you observe the future, you find a sense of exhilaration and eagerness and start to convert the quick image into a present reality. However, this generally takes much longer than the initial vision of the future. This opening into the future can also be touched as you become fully aware of your family and friends and dwell upon the miracle of the relationships and your world and how it seems to extend unendingly into the future. This world is also touched by the lovers in their higher state of first love as they see the world that might be.

To fully learn from someone else, there must be an opening to finding a oneness with the source of the teaching. This is expressed, to a degree, with the common statements that you "know where someone is coming from" or that you "know what they are attempting to say." It is as if you must first find validity in a teacher before you can fully open to him or her. Teachers of children and animal handlers know that they must first have the respect of their pupils or subjects and that the respect comes from some deep inner state of being or intention. Another awareness of this is encountered in those people who speak with authority such that the listeners know the truth of their statements without judgment.

How is oneness found or how is the mysterious state of *agapao* to be obtained?

The answer is probably best exemplified again with the state of first love. In first love, as opposed to romanticizing, there is the surrender of the self unto a complete trust in the power of the other. You allow yourself to overpower the other person and at the same time allow yourself to be overpowered by the other person. You become both dominating and dominated. This interesting state is found fairly often in conversations or activities with others where there is a clear and agreed upon goal such as attempting to understand some philosophical point or to work in unison to accomplish some physical task. The result is often described as losing yourself, being overwhelmed, taken over, completely engulfed in it, a loss of self and of control, or of the feeling of stepping into a dream. This state is characterized by the loss of self-importance, ego, and judgment. It is evidenced with the strong sensation of self-confidence in whatever you are called upon to do. There is no concern for failure or of doing wrong. There is also the need to fully give of yourself more and more without reservation.

There is a controlled aspect of the mind that many assume is the same as oneness that needs to be discussed. This is what is commonly called single-minded concentration upon some problem or task. Those who learn this type of concentration can become impervious to the outer world as they sink deeper into the object of their concentration. You have no doubt experienced this type of concentration as your mind centers upon some intriguing problem or attraction.[22] In this state your world shrinks until only the object of concentration exists and then if the object of your concentration is seen without any of your biases or expectation then a deeper form of concentration[23] results.

Many early cultures used this type of intense concentration as preparation for finding oneness. Buddhism and other religions carried this type of advanced concentration throughout many countries where it was called *meditation*. The main object of beginning meditation is to learn to bring the mind under control so as to ignore all of the distracting thoughts that keep arising. Meditation then leads to the ability to

---

[22] See *Dharana* in Glossary; Peck (1976), Ch. 6.
[23] See *Dhyana* in Glossary; Peck (1976), Ch. 7.

direct the mind outward without the normal judgments and desire for egocentricity.

Oneness is not something that you do, but rather is the result of what you are or what you are expecting. Oneness is found in losing yourself rather than in controlling yourself. Oneness requires quickening and the inner power, but not conscious effort.

5. Ecstasy

Ecstasy is associated with ever-increasing pleasure that forces you to lose the ability to control your thoughts or actions as you surrender to the increasing forces of pleasure. The chief characteristic of ecstasy is that the intensity of pleasure continually increases without satisfying the desires of the body and mind. For most adults this state can be exemplified with the rising pleasure during the overpowering drive for a sexual orgasm that finally becomes so great that the ego is buried under the resulting ecstasy. It is also commonly experienced to a degree when a group gets carried away with an increasing enthusiasm for some idea. However, if the rise in drive or pleasure ceases to increase beyond some point, then ecstasy quickly diminishes and disappears.

In children, ecstasy is found in games that require more and more attention, effort and surrender to some overpowering force. Even infants demonstrate the enjoyment of increasing involvement with games such as *peek-a-boo* that start slowly and then build with an increased tempo. Childhood games must have a natural increase in pleasure if children are to become lost in them. A good example is the ring of walking children passing under the outstretched arms of a couple playing London Bridge. As the arms fall to entrap a child, squeals of extreme delight are generally heard. Games of tag or hiding are similar in that they introduce the increasing suspense and tension that can lead toward ecstasy. A common game for young children, that seems senseless to many adults, is the simple game of,

"I am going to get you!" The adult starts with making catching motions and then increases the range and intensity until finally the child is caught amid much squirming and delight.

As you grow older, the ability to surrender is generally lost with the conditioning of society. Surrendering is replaced with yielding, compromising, or resignation. The power of the future to interact upon the individual is very different in both instances. For instance, a child surrenders with ecstasy in being forced to dig a hole as a slave in an imaginary game but finds only boredom and hardship in resigning herself to clean her room. In the first case, the game provides the controlling power, and in the second case, the parents provide the controlling power. What is the difference?

Ecstasy is found in surrendering completely to what is called an inner power. The inner power is the power that is shared in a game or interactions with others under a common goal or dedication. It is the power that is described by early religions as being associated with a personal indwelling god as will be discussed later. Your personal game is energized by your inner power as opposed to the outer power of society and institutions. The inner power is sensed as personal or that you have some hidden connection or input to it.

The inner power is recognized as guiding you through your immediate problems or challenges toward a goal, and once this power is accepted as being personal, it can be surrendered to. With the surrender ecstasy can be approached. The personal nature of the inner power can be directly compared to children finding ecstasy in play when obviously the power of the game is not considered to be threatening. However, you generally cannot find ecstasy in arguing against a stubborn person, or a computerized program, or when the controlling power is perceived as remote. You can only surrender to a power that is immediate and interactive with you and not to an alien, remorseless, uncaring, unlimited source (such as a strict parent or the government). This can be stated as playing your own game versus someone else's game. In responding to an alien power, you can only become resigned to doing that which you are required to do. It should be noted, however, that resignation to an alien power might still produce some pleasure (but not ecstasy) if it reduces rebellion, worry, indecision, and fear. For instance, some individuals resign themselves to facing a cruel and unjust world and, in that resignation, find some relief and pleasure.

In the process of surrendering, there is an increase in the inner quickening as the event approaches. As an example, near-death experiences have an increase in interest, activity, awareness, sensuality and mental acuity rather than the more normal loss of quickening associated with dying. The realization that you are dead provides a release and ecstasy rather than fear or regret.[24] Children, again, love to play games in which

---

[24] Nietzsche (1954); Personal experience

they are sacrificed, die or are placed under some imaginary restraint, much to the consternation of observing parents. The image of becoming someone dying to save others becomes an ecstatic experience to children (and to some adults).

Adults lose the ability to reach for ecstasy in simple games and instead must resort to other means of finding some form of a personal, overwhelming power. Many indigenous villages or fundamentalist groups, for instance, use ritual, fatigue, drugs, music, dance, pain or monotonous repetitions to diminish thinking or conscious control and then encourage an increase in body motions and free visualizations. This process may lead to ecstasy as ever-increasing pleasure is found in the body and mind as individuals surrender to the controlling power of the game. This surrender can again be compared to the trust and power within the game of a child. The runner's high is akin to this as the runner forces the body to continue to move despite pain and fatigue. This continues until the mind becomes overtaken with the power of the rhythm of the stride or breathing coupled with the ever-increasing fatigue. Since the power comes from the runner's own dedication, it is not feared and is certainly personal.

Ecstasy requires quickening to force the body and mind to exceed their normal control limits. One of the surprising aspects of increasing pleasure is that you must continually apply a special energy to it. You have experienced this perhaps at a party when you have decided that you are going to enjoy yourself and then force yourself to start a conversation. The conversation can become ever more pleasurable as the individuals open to it more fully. However, rather than being able to sit back and enjoy the pleasure, you know that you must keep exerting yourself even as you become lost in the wonderful feelings that arise. Reaching for ecstasy requires inner quickening to become more fully alive.

One generally unrecognized obstacle to ecstasy is the problem of allowing yourself to experience pleasure. There is a common fear of feeling good because that can only lead to something bad. A typical reaction in experiencing pleasure is to resist it since it won't last and may open the individual up to some reverse negative reactions. Our culture conditions its members to be emotionally stable and that emotional swings are dangerous with possible negative repercussions. Western schools, for instance, are attempting to allow only group emotions, well controlled by a teacher, and to suppress disturbing individual emotions such as outburst of joy, anger, frustration or intolerance.

Modern citizens are, however, easily swayed emotionally as they listen to respected authorities, since they can relax their controls in their presence. Some charismatic speakers take advantage of this reduction in emotional control to enforce their message. The speaker will generally start upon some item that is of general interest and then change the emotional content such as individual pride or shame. The speaker then swings the emotion of the listeners to, perhaps, a sense of irritation. As the audience swings from pride to irritation, they then become more open to another emotion such as fear. From fear or other such emotions, the audience needs to swing in the opposite direction and humor is often an excellent next step. The speaker then swings the audience into other emotions and each time the audience swings further and further with less and less controls until the speaker then leads them into the desired emotions that might be a religious or political form of ecstasy, outrage or fear. A group of individuals can do this to themselves many times without thought as individuals feel free to build on existing emotions until some limit is reached, and then perhaps the more controlled individual will stop the escalation with the introduction of a new topic, "to lighten the mood."

Abraham Maslow,[25] an American psychologist, describes one approach to ecstasy as a *peak experience* where there is an increase in quickening as well as a sense of union. Peak experiences are generally initiated with a strong intention to experience or to share in some higher experience with others and then continue with an exertion of energy commonly described as reaching or connecting to them. The next phase is letting yourself go, renunciation of concern for results, or surrendering to rising feelings. Perhaps the most common peak experience is encountered with the attraction for another person which can be physical, emotional, intellectual or spiritual. You find yourself

---

[25] Goble (1970), Ch. 5

attracted to the other person and then if the feelings are mutual, there is an increasing desire to share and find a union in thoughts or feelings which leads toward ecstasy.

The renunciation or sacrifice of the self, if coupled with a strong dedication, leads to the state of ecstasy that religions describe. The description of the martyrdom of saints or sages can lead the reader to some understanding of the intensity and power of this type of ecstasy. Similarly, stories are told of ancient cultures that required a virgin to give her life to save the village by jumping into a volcano or other method of sacrifice. Some American Indian stories tell about how hunters would honor the self-sacrifice of an animal so that a higher form of life could evolve.

Finding ecstasy is a strong indication that your path toward finding Heaven is the right path and not the path toward hell as you were conditioned to believe.

6. Voluptuous Nature

In our modern world today, becoming *voluptuous* is perhaps the strangest and most frightening aspect of Heaven on earth. The voluptuousness or sensuality of the body is generally more fearful than even the emotions of anger or fear. Antisthenes, an early Stoic, declared that he would rather be mad then voluptuous. This view prevails today when individuals would rather suffer than feel pleasure. As Nietzsche points out, they find pleasure in their suffering.[26] The word voluptuous perhaps is easier to understand when contrasted to the opposite feeling of being an ascetic or a stoic who suppresses the flesh. To be voluptuous is to be fully responsive to life; it is to fully enjoy the senses or the pleasures of life.

The modern world is gradually losing the simple voluptuousness of eating a plain meal or of sharing an intimate thought with others. Similarly, almost everyone is now afraid of the even more powerful voluptuousness of being touched because of the fear of losing control to someone else. There is also the fear of touching others because of their possible reactions that may result in condemnation or litigation. Individuals are, in general, also conditioned to avoid touching themselves for pleasure, even in private, primarily because of modern religious dogma that they interpret to mean that pleasure will lead to pain. In general, the members of modern society will seldom touch

---

[26] Nietzsche (1954), Aphorisms 141-142

themselves or experience or give pleasure. Many modern individuals could therefore be compared with Antisthenes and would rather be considered as cold or crazy than voluptuous.

What is the history or past usage of the term *voluptuous*? The formal meaning is quite different from its modern usage of relating to sexual deviancy or arousal. The older meaning was of "having strong visual or tactile delight." In other words, a voluptuous person can find pleasure and perhaps ecstasy in beauty and intimate contact with others. A voluptuous person is one who views a piece of art and finds an inner intense pleasure that permeates the entire body and mind. Voluptuous individuals can touch their children or spouse and become overcome by the softness, warmth and radiance of the flesh without the interposition of lust. A voluptuous person can become animated and excited with just the thought of others becoming more alive and responsive. A voluptuous individual becomes more fully alive and responsive in the presence of others with increased awareness of their physical, mental and expressive beauty.

Closely related to voluptuousness are the words *caressing* and *fondling* which are falsely used many times to describe modern socially unacceptable behavior. However, the actual meaning of these terms is quite different from being related to any sexual deviancy. Rather, both caressing and fondling are found to be very important in child rearing and social interaction. A young child historically was fondled with great pleasure both to the person fondling as well as to the child. In fact, an infant who is not fondled quickly becomes sick and dies, so fondling appears to be a very necessary part in human interactions. Women report an extreme pleasure in sexual foreplay that consists primarily of caressing and fondling. Many psychologists studying sexual behavior believe that foreplay may increase the fertility of a couple and hence is probably of some biological importance. As mentioned earlier, as adults become animated with some common experience such as an exciting discussion, they tend to move closer together and begin touching each other which increases some mode of basic communication. Touching is also well cited in the healing arts where a tender and probing touch may do more than many drugs.

Changes in the meanings of voluptuousness may be easier to understand by considering the modern changes in the meanings of sensuality, which is a form of voluptuousness. Sensuality has shifted from being related to the physical sensory enjoyment of others or self to the wearing of cosmetics, clothes, perfumes and other personal products. A modern sensual woman, for instance, presents the image that she likes the appearance of her body and its adornments. A modern sensual person is also very much aware of the correctness of what others might wear or how they wear it.

This different aspect of modern sensuality of what others wear and how they look is also extended to what is called being sensual to the feelings or viewpoints of others. In other words, in the modern world, a sensual person is very conscious of what is worn, how it is worn as well as expected feelings associated with interpersonal relationships.

Another variation of sensuality is with the modern word of *caring*. A modern sensual person *cares*, but this caring means being tolerant, considerate or charitable, all of which result from being very self-centered and judgmental. It is not interactive, but rather the impressing of care upon another, much as a farmer cares for his animals. Caring is, however, essential in a society that requires a continual concern for behavior and actions of others.

Many modern self-help groups use an older positive form of sensual activities as a method of introducing higher feelings between members of a group. These activities may start with a simple hugging of each other and then continue on to activities such as folk dancing with arms around each other's shoulders. Voluptuous activities are also introduced in workshops for couples to increase their sensuality. This may start with the simple act of touching each other's face. The surprising aspect of these workshops is that couples have to learn how and when to touch each other.

In contrast with the modern concept of sensuality that can be changed according to social demand, true voluptuousness is a very basic attribute and need of the body and mind. Voluptuousness is not, however, a permanent attribute but rather diminishes with maturity and aging unless it is kept sensitized and active. Married couples experience decreasing physical interest in each other quite soon after marriage and may look for external sexual stimulation from the various media or even from outside relationships. There are, however, some exercises that can stimulate the quickening, even in the aged, which can in turn stimulate the sense of voluptuousness and even strong sexual-like feelings.[27]

There are two separate methods of experiencing voluptuousness. The first is the intentional reaching for voluptuousness with physical, mental or spiritual self-stimulation while the second is the surrendering to external stimulation.

Voluptuousness is first found and experienced physically because it feels so good. Young children, for instance, learn that they can stimulate themselves to find feelings similar to those found when being caressed and fondled by adults. This form of self-stimulation is quite obvious as the child rubs, rocks, or strokes his body, which is sometimes an embarrassment to parents. Mental stimulation is also encountered quite early with dreaming and imagination, but spiritual stimulation is seldom encountered in young children.

---

[27] Peck (1985), II Elaboration on the Basics *Vitality*; Peck (1998), Ch. 19-22

Spiritual stimulation is commonly associated with religious practices or experiences where a spirit, god or force is assumed to enter into an individual and possesses or overpowers the worshipper. Once this occurs, then it can be recreated through the remembrance of the possession and then the submission or surrender to the feelings which then allows the experiencing of voluptuousness. The problem with this type of spiritual practice is that the wrong image or force can be worshipped without any great results. This is common with individuals who listen to Mozart's music, for instance, during some contemplation and then credit his music with the increased sensuality and ecstasy rather than the subject of their contemplation. Contemplating upon his music later might assist in finding some good feelings, but not the full sense of surrender, voluptuousness and ecstasy found during the first encounter.

External stimulation is found with the common experience of becoming overwhelmed with the intensity of some person who is best described as radiant, powerful and beautiful. The physical reaction to this type of an encounter is commonly described as the other person "took your breath away." The external power of stimulation is also sensed in such things as seeing the infinitude of a bright starry sky or being carried to some strange state of mind when fully becoming absorbed in the woods or ocean shore. You may have experienced the rise in voluptuousness as you entered into a conversation with someone who initially appeared to be quite homely and uninteresting, yet as the conversation proceeded, the other person became very attractive and beautiful.

The description of religious or mystical experiences is commonly filled with voluptuous references. The beginning of such experiences generally is described as the sensation of being overpowered, not by a threatening force, but by some soft, penetrating, vibrant, loving, warm, and comforting presence. Similarly, the body becomes soft as a child's: new, rejuvenated, filled with life and sensuality. This state of physical well-being was related to being in a feminine state or as the ancients would state, being controlled by the inner moon.

There is the counter masculine nature of voluptuousness or the experiencing of the inner power of the sun that needs at least a brief discussion. As the body and mind become overpowered in some powerful interaction, beautiful scene, thought or state of *agapao*,[28] there can be a strong rising of a drive to reach out, merge with or become physically and mentally one with the source of the interaction. Since this sensation is opposite to the opening or surrendering experience, it is considered to be masculine.

Some individuals encounter this state during an impending disaster such as a car skidding out of control or in such cases as rescuing someone else from instant

---

[28] See *Agapao* in Glossary; Peck (1999), Ch. 3.

harm. The body feels empowered and capable of meeting any demand, time stands still, and every sense is active. You feel completely alive and responsive. Later it is not uncommon to find that you seemed to have slightly leaked urine and that there is a strong sexual feeling in your groin that is quite masculine in feeling. Some Eastern schools describe this sensation as being due to the stimulation of an inner *Shiva Linga* organ that exists in the lower abdomen and releases a fluid called *soma*. This type of voluptuousness or reaction has no support from the modern world and requires a great deal of discussion well beyond the capability of this book.[29]

Because of the ignorance of sensuality and the mistrust of its powers, voluptuousness decreases in individuals with each generation as well as within each lifetime. If the senses are not constantly used, the sensory responses decrease so that the magnitude of sensual experience also decreases and the voluptuous nature is gradually lost. This can be described as resulting from the continual diminishing of the sensitivity of the body and its senses through the gradual degeneration of the nerves and sensory organs through disuse. Nevertheless, this loss can be reversed at any age by regular stimulation that may, however, require many months to more fully develop the sensitivity and responses.

---

[29] Peck (1998), Ch. 9

There is also another very interesting aspect of voluptuousness and that is its development does not appear to have any final limitations.[30] Voluptuousness is an enveloping element of Heaven that can continually increase the joy and thrill in this life and beyond.

---

[30] Ibid.

7. Rebirth

The word *rebirth* sometimes conveys the fundamentalist Christian concept of being *saved* or of becoming a member of a church. There is also, however, the ancient concept of becoming a different person in a different world which is the subject of this chapter. The term rebirth is perhaps better explained using some Eastern terms such as *liberated, freed* or *enlightened* where an individual is freed from social conditioning. This is similarly expressed in some Western religions as the state of an individual who is able to see, hear, and respond to the actual truth of life. The reborn individual actually becomes a different person in responding to the outer world and this transformation may be of short duration or a continuing change throughout life.

Western religions generally equate rebirth to a higher state of mind and body although many individuals do find a rebirth into a lower state of existence of increased bondage to conditioning. However, this book will consider only the rebirth into a more evolved world.

Rebirth is a result of the shift from responding to the conditioned forces of society to quickening and the inner power. These inner forces become activated by an immediate demand to become a different person or from a long-range dedication to evolve into another person. The couple in first love is an excellent starting illustration. Initially they feel so wonderful together that they are able to ignore much of their conditioning as to what they are supposed to be or do. They are able, to some extent, to find their own world and create their own direction to travel. They are not concerned about being what they are supposed to be, but rather, attempt to be the reflection of the other. Since they are able to shift their view of the world from how they were supposed to see it to what they need to see, their outer world changes considerably to an ever-increasing joy and trust. This shift immediately changes their relationship to others and also their view of the future. It should be noted that their new world is built upon their old world and is generally supportive of the old world instead of being oppositional or destructive.

Rebirth into Heaven is not obtained with simple rebelling against society nor by separating yourself from society or even by feeling superior to others and society. Further, this rebirth is not obtained by joining a group to which you must become further conditioned as to belief and social interaction. Such actions only result in becoming further bonded to conditioning. An example of group bondage is found within teenage cliques where peer pressure to conform becomes the overriding control. Interestingly, this bondage generally does result in a rebirth, but not into Heaven.

Rebirth into Heaven results in the changing of your relationship to society. Instead of being dependent upon society or of competing against it, you find that you build or stand upon it. Society and its evolution are perceived to offer great support for further perfection of the self rather than denigration of the self. You become free to use the wisdom, materials, resources and interactions with others as tools to seek and find your own goals in life, rather than letting them limit your expression of life. As one Eastern expression states it, "You are *in* the world rather than *of* the world." By not being *of* the world, you also become non-judgmental of the world and hence free.

Rebirth starts with the realization that you have a control over your own future and that with proper effort and dedication you can reach any dedicated goal. You find that the path toward that goal will be pleasant, rewarding, exciting and increasingly ecstatic. Rebirth requires the trust that each step along the path will be guided by the power of the goal or by a higher perfecting power.[31] Nietzsche stated it as, "Man becomes that which he wants to be; his volition precedes his existence."[32] This trust is reflected in the old commandment of loving (*agapao*) God with your heart, soul, and might. Without this surrender to a higher guiding power, coupled with the exertion of discerning and following each step, rebirth and consequently Heaven cannot be attained.

Rebirth into Heaven is found in people of many different ages. Children can suddenly change their ways and become new and exciting individuals. In middle age many creative individuals who have mastered their world may drastically change their roles.

---

[31] Proverbs 16:9 "Man sets his direction, but God controls the steps."

[32] Nietzsche (1954), Aphorism 39

Religions often describe deathbed conversions in old age. Trauma or an intense love are known to transform people of all ages. Religious experiences that present the vision of new worlds or states of consciousness generally are also associated with rebirth.

There is also a temporary state of rebirth wherein an individual becomes something different such as found in an extremely demanding situation. This is exemplified with stories such as that of a small lady suddenly becoming a super person to rescue a child, or an individual suddenly becoming filled with compassion and an insight into the needs of a suffering stranger encountered on the street.

Actors and actresses find a temporary state of rebirth (as do children playing make-believe) into new roles that are quite different from their *normal* roles. Professionals tend to do this every working day as they step into some authoritative role. You may deliberately seek a rebirth from being a weak frightened person to being brave and strong as you walk down a lonely street at night.

Alcohol is known to release inhibitions such that individuals can become someone new and different. Part of the reason for serving alcohol at parties is that guests can become someone different from their normal conservative or restrictive roles. The problem with alcohol is, however, that the individual also loses the ability to choose or control the role to be played.

Rebirth is found in some social exchanges, where you might, for instance, find yourself overacting and becoming enthusiastic about some new activity that you are engaged in with others. You can remember many such instances when you became so interested in what was going to happen that you forgot who or what you were and became some entirely different person as you reached for more involvement in the oncoming moment. The role that you put on was, however, perfect for the manifesting of your desire. You might normally be timid and reserved, but when faced with some topic with individuals you trust and perhaps admire, you can become a very intelligent and clear spoken person, perfectly capable of making your views quite clear to others. Later you probably questioned what came over you or possessed you to become so different and what they thought of you.

This book is concerned principally with the rebirth that accompanies the change in yourself as you meet some desired goal in life. In general, you find yourself becoming different as you put your quickening into some oncoming experience while you also forget the concerns of the self, judgments of others, and simply trust in the outcome.

The concern for the self and what others might think is, as mentioned before, an obstacle to reaching Heaven. However, it is amazing how once the concern is dropped, your new role and self both become far more acceptable as well as powerful in your interactions. It is as if you can become a perfect person to interact with others in accordance with your dedication. This phenomenon is similar to the elderly lady who becomes whatever is required to save a child or the change that occurs within you as you overcome basic fears in order to accomplish some purpose.

Rebirth into Heaven can, therefore, be characterized as becoming the perfected person to accomplish some dedicated task. The rebirth is not intentional, although the desire to accomplish the task must be very intentional such that you become vitalized. This change also requires sufficient faith in the future to allow the rebirth to take place. The rebirth is also accompanied with the sense of ecstasy or craziness that overrides the mind with the loss of concern. The body and mind seem voluptuous and fully responsive to interactions with others. It is easily expressed as being in Heaven.

Rebirth is a continual process in life as you seek to become more perfected in fully living your unfolding life. This becoming ever more perfected is easily seen as you become aware of your world opening up or that you are facing more and more challenges that must be met. The fact that you can view a constant improvement and power in your life is why it is described by the ancients as a dedicated path with each step being an unknown, although the direction is quite obvious from extrapolating from the past.

8. The Inner Power Behind Heaven

There is a general acceptance of the concept that the great people of society are able to draw from and exhibit special inner powers. Religions assure their members that they too can find a higher power when they are called upon to meet the demands of life but that certain requirements must first be met. Most early religious writings also point out that only a few are able to find the source of this power and in the Judaic/Christian religions those few are called the *righteous* and do not require further teachings. The other agreement of religions is that those who deny the existence of this inner power will find death.

Most religions suggest that the inner power is not only the source of the five elements of Heaven on earth but also furnishes the guidance through the steps of life. Because of the broad range of the inner power, the source of this power is generally described as coming from an indwelling god, divine spirit, inner presence, or metaphysical power source.

Jesus called the source of the inner power, *father*, which was a metaphysical term, similar to *lord* or *indwelling god* as used in other cultures, and he argued that its existence was evidenced by the creative works which came forth from it.[33] The modern scientific or materialistic world has no better argument or explanation, since the origin of creativity as well as

---

[33] Matthew, Ch. 5-7

supernormal feats have no physical explanation. There is no test to prove that an individual is creative or being guided by the inner power other than by observing his or her works. Creative works must be more than doing good, the redistribution of resources, duty, or social responsibilities. For a work to be creative, it must in a true sense violate the law of entropy.[34] The works of a righteous person have never been described nor are they expected.[35]

Since the inner power is manifested by the righteous or evolved individuals, it seems reasonable to study them so as to perhaps learn more about the inner power. The most recent efforts have been undertaken by Maslow[36] who summarized to some degree the much earlier Eastern studies such as done by the Yoga, *Tantra* or *Tao* schools who also studied superior individuals. Maslow found, in agreement with the ancient concepts, that before perfection can be found, a basic hierarchy of needs has to be met. These basic needs start with maintaining the health of the body, then developing the mind, followed by the mastering of social skills and interactions. A very few of those who master the basic needs are then able to work toward and find perfection. Maslow called these few the *self-actualized, fully human* or *superior persons*. Frank G. Goble[37] noted that the characteristics that Maslow associated with the

---

[34] Peck (1998), Ch.4 and Ch.5
[35] *Gospel of Thomas*, Verse 2
[36] Goble (1970), Maslow (1993), Maslow (1954)
[37] Goble (1970), Ch. 3

self-actualized persons corresponded directly to those described by religions as the *righteous*, *perfected*, *liberated* or *saved* individuals or those who managed to find Heaven on earth.

The characteristics of the righteous as universally described can be summarized as:

1. seeing life as it really is,
2. knowing or truly seeing others without bias,
3. finding their own sense of right and wrong,
4. understanding what is behind the manifest,
5. being unaffected by common desires,
6. having strong dedications,
7. enjoying each moment of life particularly during opposition or challenge,
8. being highly creative,
9. lacking fear,
10. having weak self-conflicts, and
11. forming deep and long-lasting relationships.

The righteous are fully aware of their inner power and trust and rely upon it. According to the early writings, one of the more important attributes of the righteous individuals is the ability to determine what is right and wrong. The rights and wrongs that these perfected individuals find are in complete agreement with those expounded by religious edicts around the world. These *self-actualized* individuals do not need to rely upon social or religious law, but find it within themselves. Both Jesus and earlier Indian documents state how the righteous or perfected individual does not need religious instruction but already knows the teachings.

Nietzsche[38] gave a practical explanation of how exceptional persons strengthen their mores, social instinct and goodness by finding the pleasure associated with proper actions. The superior persons, because of their gained experience and knowledge from seeking pleasure, finally know what is honorable and profitable for themselves as well as others.

Society and its conditioned members are, however, very suspicious of anyone who claims to act upon inner guidance or prompting rather than social law. This fear is well-grounded since immature, neurotic, or psychotic individuals can do tremendous harm to themselves as well as to others as they follow some inner prompting. Further, most individuals are afraid of quieting the judgmental brain and allowing some unknown force to direct their actions. They are well aware of how they can become irrational when they encounter intense emotional confrontations and the normal controls seem to disappear. There is another source of anxiety and that is with the religious or political extremists who claim to have an inner

---

[38] Nietzsche (1954), Aphorisms 94-98

guidance as they initiate social unrest, hatred, violence or destruction.

The above antisocial behavior can be easily explained as arising from a sense of being above or uncaring for the laws of society. The righteous, on the other hand, never claim to be above the law, but rather accept the necessity of social law as a foundation for growth. This is why the path toward finding Heaven first requires the mastery of the social world. Effectuating a change in society requires a thorough understanding of society as well as its processes. To become a superior person in society, a union with society is required rather than an opposition. The inner guidance cannot, therefore, be at odds with the stability of society.

Maslow and Nietzsche can be seen as explaining that the laws of a society are logical and supportable and have proven to be functional over many years of existence. A superior or righteous individual, being intelligent, would be expected to also live by them and even follow them more closely than an undeveloped individual. As for instance, a wise or developed person will obey traffic laws and knows that to queue up in a line is efficient. The wise person knows that social laws, such as table manners, make social interactions easier and pleasant. Similarly, there is an intense joy in assisting and instructing others so that a superior person can be expected to serve his society. A righteous person can also be seen as being so busy in working toward a long-range goal in life that there is little attraction for spending effort on petty desires such as obtaining revenge or seeking security. Instead, the righteous know that the greater the challenge, the greater the rewards and that the happier they make others, the happier they become.

Concerning personal goals, the earlier studies of evolved or righteous individuals suggested that an individual arrives into this world with some basic goals already in place. Parents sometimes sense this as some children are obviously born with a purpose in life, and early in their life they manifest their inner power to fulfill that purpose. Other children can be perceived as finding a purpose later in childhood as they become obsessed with some direction they wish to travel.

Some adults are aware of some deep sense of a desired direction they would like to travel during their life or the sense of some goal to attain but recognize that they have difficulty in keeping on their path. They are too easily distracted by their desires and fears and seem to lack an inner fire to fully expand their life. They also become aware, however, of an inner voice or feeling that counters opposing distractions. If this inner unrest and voice increase with living their life and becomes the source of an ever-increasing sense of a lack of fulfillment, then they are awakening to the possibility of becoming righteous. It is to these individuals that the early sages and saints addressed their teachings stressing the two different worlds of the sinners and the righteous.

Unfortunately, the teachings were glossed over by those individuals who were not aware of the true subject of the teachings as will be evidenced in the next chapter. A similar distortion of the teachings is illustrated in a Chinese parable that reads only, "The finger pointing at the moon." The teaching of this simple parable is that you can become attracted to the finger rather than the object that it is directing the mind toward. This has occurred in almost all of the world's religions where the pointing fingers have become revered, worshipped, and fought over, and the universal truths that the fingers pointed to are ignored, distorted or forgotten.

When the original teachings are fully explored without social interpretation, they can be seen as describing an inner power that leads and guides you toward experiencing and trusting in an ever increasing demanding and rewarding life.

To listen and respond to the inner power, there must be a disregard for or renunciation of all that you think that you know so that you can become open to the unknown future. To listen, the conditioned conscious brain must be quieted with all of its commands, counter commands and judgments. This can be done by mastering two different controls. The first control is to forcibly quiet the mind through inner thought control techniques that require the concentrating of the mind upon some object that can become so pleasurable or attractive that the thoughts are ignored.[39] The second control is similar except that a goal is concentrated upon to such an extent that each moment becomes a reflection of it and changes your view of the old conditioned world.[40] Only the exciting and evolutionary is perceived, even if the brain calls it work or unpleasant.

The first approach can be facilitated with Eastern or early Judaic/Christian practices called meditation or contemplation. The second approach requires the activation of the body and its senses through practices such as used to increase the source of quickening which can be found in both Eastern and early Western practices.

The inner power to create your own Heaven on earth must start with the mastery of society as a sinner and then obtaining a strong dedication to rise above society which can then awaken the inner forces and lead you into righteousness.

---

[39] Peck (1976), Ch. 6; Peck (1994) II. Slokas and commentaries in Practices
[40] Ibid., Ch. 7

9. Early Writings on Heaven on Earth

Early religious writings from around the world describe life at two levels or within two different worlds, that of the sinners and that of the righteous. The sinners are the majority of individuals who are dominated and controlled by their social conditioning. The source of their sins is described in many different models as being the power of darkness, ignorance, controlling spirits, or the sins of Adam. The model of the sins of Adam, as being the chief obstacle to finding Heaven, can certainly be accepted in modern times. Modern psychology, for instance, generally places the source of an individual's social problems on his parents and early home life, but those parents had to have gained those same problems from their parents who gained them from their parents and so on back to Adam.

The second level of life consists of those righteous few who are able to break free of the bondage of the teachings of parents and society and find a more perfect path through life. They find their path with a strong dedication of where they desire to go and a trust in a special inner power to strengthen and guide them. The inner power opens the individual to experiencing a new world that is built upon the old, yet having added features that could not be seen before. For instance, strangers, rather than being seen as objectionable, can be seen as a source of truth. Challenges in life become gifts rather than punishments. The body becomes a source of pleasure and a tool for exploring new sensations instead of being an unhealthy, dying, obscene collection of distractions. The thoughts of the mind become stimulating and exciting rather than dangerous and threatening. The future in the new world is an opening rather than a closing.

The righteous who dwell in Heaven on earth have also been called by various names such as the awakened, perfected beings, the elite of God, and liberated by the many religious writings that describe them. It is very interesting that the majority of the early writings describe this special inner power as coming forth from an inner chamber, center, vault, cauldron, or room located within the seekers, deep within their bowels.

Within this inner vault or chamber resides the source of the special power that is also credited with perfect wisdom and knowledge given to the seeker. There is no model or worldly description that can be applied to this inner source and hence the description becomes allegorical or symbolic in literary writings. Because of its strong personal characteristics, the inner power was generally described as coming forth from an indwelling spirit, god or gods. For instance, to the Jews the source of the power was commonly attributed to *Adonai* or Lord; to the Christians, it was called *Christ* or the *Spirit of Christ*. The early descriptions in the *Vedas* describe the inner power as coming forth from many gods and goddesses depending upon the particular manifested power. The modern materialist might describe the source as an inner intuition, gut feeling or the subconscious mind.

Describing the higher form of life to the majority who have never experienced Heaven on earth is nearly impossible, so many of the old writings resort to myths. The problem of describing the higher form of life or Heaven was summarized by a modern sage of India, Ramakrishna, who stated that it was like attempting to describe how candy tasted to someone who had never tasted sugar.

As an example of a myth used to describe the inner power, consider the Indian *Bhagavad Gita*[41] (which literally means the "Song of Speaking with the Beloved"). The song presents the model of the inner soul of an individual as a warrior riding within a chariot which symbolizes the outer physical body. Horses, depicting the power of the body to interact with the world, pull the chariot. The chariot also contains a charioteer, *Krishna*, representing the source of the inner power who is able to expertly control the horses and guide the chariot (however, only when called upon to do so.) The story reaches its climax as the inner *Krishna* demonstrates his powers and love that overwhelms the soul of the individual. The soul then finds oneness (or speaks) with *Krishna* and then agrees to let *Krishna* control the horses and direct the chariot to find the agreed upon goal.

Both the Judaic and Christian writings ignore the philosophy of the inner power and rather speak of the

---

[41] Besant (1987)

righteous[42] who inhabit the Heaven on earth and evidence the inner power primarily by their works. Their works are generally well above what others could do and contain sufficient creativity so that an open mind can perceive the greatness within them and know that it is from the Lord. In contrast to the righteous are the vast numbers of the sinners who are nonetheless to be rewarded by a Heaven outside and above themselves for any singular righteous acts. This is perhaps illustrated within the third chapter of Malachi in the Bible which states that if tithes are paid then the window of heaven will be opened so that blessings can flow down.

Jesus refers to the Heaven on earth as the *Kingdom of Heaven* (or the *Kingdom of God*) and tells his followers that this kingdom is near and can be found by those who earnestly seek it during their lifetime. Jesus continues to support the Judaic concept of the righteous who are excluded from needing to follow his teachings. He introduces this idea with his statement:

"They that are whole have no need of the physician, but they that are sick."

"I came not to call the righteous, but sinners to repentance."[43]

_____

[42] See *Righteous* in Glossary.
[43] Matthew 9:12; Matthew 9:13; See also I Timothy 1:9.

The Book of Psalms in the Bible is concerned primarily with the reward that the righteous receive from the Lord with perhaps the Twenty-third Psalm being considered a classic example of being in Heaven on earth. The characteristics of *oneness*, *quickening*, *ecstasy*, *voluptuousness*, the promise of *rebirth*, and an *eternal life* can be readily seen in the psalm presented below.

Twenty-third Psalm

The Lord is my shepherd; I shall not want.
He makes me to lie down in green pastures;
he leads me beside the still waters.

He restores my soul: he leads me
in the paths of righteousness
for his name's sake.
Yea, though I walk through
the valley of the shadow of death,
I will fear no evil: for thou art with me;
thy rod and thy staff they comfort me.

Thou prepares a table before me
in the presence of mine enemies:
thou anoints my head with oil; my cup runs over.
Surely goodness and mercy shall follow me
all the days of my life: and I will dwell
in the house of the Lord forever.

Confusion exists in describing God the creator and the personal Lord. Many individuals who attempt to explain that there is only one God or that they are both the same have trouble arguing that a Creator God is also concerned about their petty problems. To obtain a possible clearer understanding of the usage of the Judaic/Christian word *Lord*, the Judaic definition of God can be clarified. The Bible can be seen to distinguish three different forms of God:

- The first form, called *Elohim*, is impossible to love since it is the remote God or Gods who created the universe and is unknowable.

- The second nature of God as *Jehovah* is easily seen as the maintainer of the world as well as the director of the future evolution of the world. *Jehovah* is difficult to understand or love since *Jehovah* is inseparable from the activities of the entire world.

- The third nature of God that can be loved is *Adonai* or Lord that is a personal enveloping and directing power that acts in the immediate moment. It is *Adonai* that is felt as an inner source of truth, comfort, surety, knowledge or energy that pours forth when required. This inner source of power comes forth uncontrolled by the conscious mind and changes your world. *Adonai* is also easy to identify with what the later Christians called the *Spirit of Christ*. It is this form of the Divine that is felt as a personal guide or power that leads you into the Kingdom of Heaven.

It is interesting to note that many other religions also have the same three forms of God expressed in similar ways but called different names.

In looking for scriptural descriptions or discussions of the inner power and Heaven on earth, a surprising obstacle is found in many of the translations or interpretations of religious writings from around the world. These translations or interpretations replace only a few key words with other meanings that subtly but very effectively change the content of the original writings. As will be demonstrated later, a change in meaning of just a few critical words can change the entire understanding of a document.

It is difficult to accept a switch back to the original meaning of a word that has been changed and then ingrained into your mind over most of your life. As a simple example, the average reader probably still has trouble considering the word *righteous* to mean a perfected or superior being instead of someone who follows church dogma. It is therefore better to present further examples of the changes in words as used in other languages before introducing the changes in critical English words.

As an introduction to the change in the meaning of critical words consider the ten words considered to be rules of conduct called the *Yamas* and *Niyamas* given to *Hatha Yoga* students. Yoga students are told of six of the ancient terms which tell them that they must be:

1. Non-violent
2. Truthful
3. Non-stealing
4. Non-coveting
5. Pure
6. Content

Few individuals would disagree with the meanings of these six terms. However, the other four terms of the *Yamas* and *Niyamas* have a singularly biased religious nature which will be shown to be the result of changing the literal meaning of the original descriptive words. The following table lists these four Sanskrit words (from the *Yamas* and *Niyamas*), the popular translation and the probable original meaning. The Glossary can be consulted for the full explanation of the derivation of the meanings from the Sanskrit.

Sanskrit	**Popular**	**Original**
Tapas	Austerity	Being fervent.
Svadhyana	Study scripture	Aware of inner forces.

| *Isvara Pranidhana* | Think of God | Aware of inner guidance. |
| *Bramacharya* | Chastity | Following inner guidance. |

The severe consequence of the change in the meaning of the words is obvious once the original meaning of the words is accepted and the conditioned response to the words ignored. The modified meaning of the words can also be clearly seen as supporting a religious interpretation or dogma. What is of interest is that the apparent original meanings describe the importance of the lower heart and inner power.

One ancient school of India has suffered much condemnation, and because of the false interpretation of its description of Heaven on earth, has become a support for later schools of eroticism that are completely contrary to its original teachings. The average educated Indian may well find an immediate distaste at the mention of this school, namely *Tantra*.

Consider the common offered proof of the eroticism of *Tantra* that dwells on five words which all start with the letter "M" in the following Table.[44]

---

[44] See *Pancamakara* in *Glossary*.

Sanskrit	Popular	Original
Matsya	Eating fish	Quickening, Pisces
Maithuna	Having sex	Union, Coupled
Madya	Drinking alcohol	Oneness, Ecstatic
Mansa	Eating meat	Voluptuous, Flesh
Mudra	Eating aphrodisiacs	New Person, Symbol

The difference between the original meanings of the words and the implied meanings of the opponents of *Tantra* is quite clear. The effectiveness of the shift in meanings is well evidenced today when *Tantra* is understood to be either a doctrine of prolonged sex or an evil cult. In support of the original meanings, the ancient universal usage of *fish*, to imply a higher life energy is well known.[45] It should be remembered that Hindus have always had a deep revulsion of eating meat and drinking alcohol and any evolving Hindu would certainly not indulge in such habits. Since the Yoga and *Tantra* schools of India taught that sexual orgasm depleted the inner spiritual quickening and that marriage vows were sacred, the above sex reference turned *Tantra* into an evil cult to the average Hindu. The purity of *Tantra* is, however, easily proven by reverting back to the original writings using the accepted word meanings of that time.

The original teachings of *Tantra* may well have also formed the basis for many of the late religious expressions of the nature and powers of the individual as well as the description of Heaven on earth. The word *Tantra* has an original meaning of "the means of manifesting special powers."[46]

The goal of *Tantra* was to use special techniques to reach the higher state called *anuttara* or perfection that is equivalent with this book's expression, "Heaven on earth." *Tantra* was primarily concerned with the transformed body and mind that was associated with perfected or evolved individuals (the righteous).

As an introduction to the teachings of *Tantra* consider the following condensed version of the ancient

---

[45] See discussion of *fish* on p. 8.
[46] See *Heart*, *Tantra*, *Tameion* in Glossary.

Paratrimshika[47] or *Thirty Verses.* It provides some basic definitions of terms such as *sun*, *moon*, *heart*, *heaven*, *rebirth* and *creation*, which were widely used within fundamental religious teachings of later religions of the known world.

The Paratrimshika

*The sun and moon must be
separated with special practices.*

*The power of the moon is found to exist
in the lower feminine center or heart.*

*The power of the sun is found as a
creative knowing force in the heart.
The power of the sun envisions and creates
a Heaven on earth that is to be.*

*The power removes what is not desired
from all of the possibilities.*

*As the future unfolds, the power of the moon
makes the creation manifest and real.
Heaven results with union of the sun and moon.*

*The sun principle is able to recognize
the mystical nature of matter, space, time and energy
and see them as basic building blocks for reality.*

---

[47] Peck (1998) Part E Resources Table 4; Singh (1988)

*The moon principle is filled with
the radiance of the building blocks that is
reflected in their reality.*

*The lower feminine heart is just above the perineum
and is the junction of the ruling powers
and the soul and must be activated to find Heaven.*

*When the powers of the sun and moon are combined,
an inner unseen fluid is created that flows upwards,
manifesting the ecstatic rebirth of the self.*

*The reborn self was also created in the future
and is now manifested in the present flow.
The reborn self is perceived with increased
feminine properties or as being androgynous.*

*The new self is beyond sin or blame and knows
the path to perfection without
religious training, observances or rite.
The new self now belongs to the elect.*

*The new world is controlled by the creative,
destructive and maintaining powers of the sun power.
The new world grows from the original vision as a
great tree grows from a small seed.*

*In the new world, the desire to sink into or
find oblivious or eternal rest disappears.
The upward flowing of the inner fluid
maintains the ecstasy and reality
of the new world and self.*

Whatever is desired and worked for
becomes reality, all power lies within the self.
The union of the sun and moon
is the source of all knowledge and powers.

Another later document from Egypt called the *Emerald Tablet* written by the Egyptian sage, Hermes Trismegistus, is now presented. This document is interesting since it was one of the early writings associated with the school of Alchemy that was also falsely accused of black magic and in particular the conversion of lead into gold. The obvious explanation is that rather than trying to convert lead into gold, the attempt was to convert sinners into the righteous.

The Emerald Tablet

It is true, that as it is above, so it is below.

All things are from the One,
by the One becoming Two.

The Sun is the Father, the Mother is the Moon.
The breath has carried it to the belly and
the body nurtures. The gateway to perfection is now
opened through this potential
lying in the depths of the physical.

Only with the greatest care, is the physical
separated from the subtle or the subtle
from the physical. It rises from the depths to the
heights; descends,
while the higher and lower magnify the power.

The promise is as follows:
the world in all its glory is seen with clarity and
wisdom. More powerful than strength and force,
solid and subtle are conquered,
and thus all is created, that which is,
and the perfection of tomorrow.

The meaning of this writing can be described briefly as:

- The Heaven above is like the Heaven below on earth.

- There is a central power in Heaven that is manifested as the masculine and the feminine.

- The living and vital breath activates the above forces in the body.

- The power is stored in the belly and is the potential force for perfection.

- You must learn to separate the two forces with care (to avoid conditioning).

- The inner powers are directed to rise to become manifested and magnified.

- With the rise of the inner powers, there is a rebirth into a more perfected state.

- The flow of the inner power is more powerful than all of the prior conditioning or strength of the body and mind.

- Everything that is or will be experienced is created by the lower inner power.

Perhaps it is possible to now turn to the Judaic/Christian distortions starting with the word *love*. Most Jews and Christians believe that the fundamental law in the Bible is the commandment to love God with all of your heart, soul and might, followed by loving your neighbor. The common distortion of these commandments is that you should not sin and rather do God's will by giving money to your religious institution and charities. Love is therefore simplified to the act of giving money or its equivalent. As has already been described in Chapter Four, however, the original word for love was *agapao* which implies a oneness. Another interpretation is that love toward God and your neighbor should be like the love toward family or as a brother or sister. *Agapao*, however, cannot be interpreted to mean this type of relationship and had the Bible intended to indicate this, it would have used the Greek word *philio* which means family-type love.

There are a number of stories about remote Semitic tribes that can be used to further verify the above analysis of the original usage of *agapao*. Typical stories relate how some outsider is lost in the desert and then administered to as he stumbles into a Semitic camp. The people open to him, reaching deep into his soul to discover his needs, give even their own portions of food to him, comfort him and supply him with voluptuous surroundings, vitalize him and in the end of the story, he leaves this desert Heaven as a new and reformed man. This type of story can also be compared with the story that Jesus told of a good Samaritan who gave his time and effort to help a wounded stranger on a well-used highway. After determining his needs and giving him dressings, he then placed him into an inn that could further provide for his needs as he healed.

Jesus taught methods of entering the Kingdom of Heaven, yet the descriptive words have been altered over the centuries as has occurred in other religious writings. This can be explained in part by the translators of the original Greek or Aramaic not having personally experienced Heaven on earth and using translations that fit into the social or religious world of the time. It is also difficult for a person raised within a social and religious milieu to accept another meaning of a word that varies from the popular and accepted connotation, and this no doubt further hides the original meaning.

In general, the original teachings can be seen to teach of an inner power that was later shifted to a power in Heaven above. An excellent example is afforded with Matthew 6:6, a part of the famous *Sermon on the Mount*. The verse instructs the reader to first "enter into your closet." Closet is a shift of the original meaning of the Greek word *tameion* that generally referred to a lower storeroom in a house. "Shutting the door" is an Eastern expression meaning to close your mind on the outer world. "To pray to your father which is in secret" can be better understood using the following original meanings of the key words. *To pray* comes from *prosuechomal* which means to move toward the source of desire. *Father* is a universal name for the inner power. *Being in secret* is another modification of the word *tameion* as does the following statement of *seeing in secret*. The original verse can therefore be literally restated as:

"You must seek the lower room that contains the inner power that sees and rewards you."

St. John of the Cross, a famous Catholic teacher, wrote a very popular short poem entitled, *Dark Night of the Soul*[48] that is assumed to describe the above verse. (It should be noted that he later was required to write a commentary on his poem to make it compatible with church dogma.)

Below is a short paraphrase:

Dark Night of the Soul

On a dark night with intense yearning,
I put my house at rest and in concealment
and in darkness, I went forth without light
guided by the light from the secret chamber.
I found the ladder and lowered myself
into the chamber of my beloved.
A place where none appeared.

---

[48] St. John of the Cross (1959)

The night more lovely than the dawn,
joined the lover with the beloved.
He remained sleeping and I caressed him
and found my senses overpowered.
I surrendered myself and forgot my cares
in the fragrance of his presence.

A condensed and altered version of the remainder of the *Sermon on the Mount* will be given next using the literal meanings of the words that shift the meaning from the above discussions of distortions and dogma to the original religious teachings and concepts.

The *Sermon* can be seen to be a beautiful dissertation on finding Heaven on earth. The reader is encouraged to compare the following with the accepted versions, but using the literal meanings of the critical words.

From *The Other Sermon on the Mount*:[49]

* *You will be blessed by entering into the Heaven on earth when you do not attempt to control your immediate life or cling to personal desires.*

* *Accept life without judgment or resistance and you will gain this Heaven.*

* *When you find righteousness within your life, then you will find Heaven on earth.*

---

[49] Adapted from Peck (1999), Ch.16

- *You have the potential for changing the earth, but if you ignore the potential, then you find death.*

- *You have an inner Light and you must reach your summit so that it can shine from there and illuminate the darkness and be seen.*

- *As you follow your inner knowledge, people will see your great works and marvel at the inner creative power.*

- *If you wish to enter Heaven on earth, you must first be able to obey every aspect of the required social Law even more so than those representing the Laws.*

- *You must renounce any action that you do or have done that binds you to continual self-judgment or else your whole being remains locked in the lower world.*

- *Everyone is taught to love their neighbor and hate their enemy, but in Heaven on earth, you will love those who oppose or harm you and support them that speak against you.*

- *You must become outwardly as perfect as the Divine power dwelling within you.*

- *Revere and honor the power within your center of being. Let this power flow forth. With this power, judgments, guilt, and remorse disappear. There is no concern for that which we do or say since we are led by the inner light.*

- *If you can hold to that space where there are no perceived transgressions of others, then you likewise cannot transgress. If you judge and condemn others then you cannot find the inner source.*

- *When you do practices to improve yourself, do not do or modify them for others, but rather only that which is required by the inner power and need.*

- *Increase that which is in your inner lower heart. The world is formed by the manner in which it is viewed. If your vision is clear, then the whole world is crystal clear. If your view of the world is that it is evil, then your whole world and body is evil. If darkness is found within yourself, then your world is in absolute darkness.*

- *Take no thought for your life, what you will eat or drink; nor for your body, or what you will wear.*

For a comparison, excerpts from the *Gospel of Thomas* will be given. The *Gospel of Thomas* was recently found at Nag Hammadi having been sealed for centuries since its placement there by the early Gnostics. The manuscript, which is generally accepted as being older than the Gospels of the Bible, is also largely unedited since it was hidden for the intervening centuries and can more directly reflect the early teachings and concepts.

The following excerpts are changed by the author, however, to reflect the early usage of the word *Jesus* as can be evidenced by comparing the following text with the original. Jesus was used with two meanings: one is Jesus the man who brought forth Truth and the other is as the inner power that brings forth Truth. The word Jesus as used in the second sense is changed to the word *truth* to make the reading easier.

Other changes are made to update the text to the modern world and to make it more readable (the original text should be referenced for verification.) The *Gospel of Thomas* contains many verses that are nearly identical with those in the New Testament. Hence, the similar verses are not listed except for verse 107 that adds the missing piece about the lost sheep being the most valuable (for breeding) of the flock.

From the *Gospel of Thomas*:

1. *Whosoever fully understands these sayings will escape death.*

2. *Seek until it is found. That which is found is always the unexpected. The unexpected stimulates the self. Being stimulated, access to the inner Truth is gained. Then one conquers the world.*

10. *Truth is cast upon the earth as fires and although quickly extinguished by the majority, smolders over all the land.*

14. Efforts for the salvation of the self through self-denial, prayer, or charity can be detrimental to finding Heaven on earth. Rather be open to anyone who would speak or interact with you. What goes into the body cannot poison, only that which comes forth in words and deeds.

22. Truth is not in the Two, neither in the good nor bad, the just or unjust, the female nor the male. Only when the Two are separated and then made into One, can the Kingdom of Heaven be entered.

23. Those with Truth are the elite. One out of a thousand, two out of ten thousand, yet they shall ever be One.

26. Find the Light within your Self and then clear your vision, only then can you see to assist others.

37. Truth can only be fully received when you can freely reveal your nakedness as a child.

41. Those who can grasp accomplishment will gain more. Those with nothing of gain will lose the little they have.

45. A man of Truth is not without accomplishment. A man of evil has little of value.

51. When will the renewal of the world come? It is here but unrecognized.

55. *When family and filial responsibilities can be set aside and forgotten, Truth can be sought and found.*

58. *There is evolution in suffering if it leads to the Light.*

69. *Blessed are those who find inner doubts and conflicts about themselves. In seeking resolution, Truth is found. Blessed are they who hunger for Light, for they shall find Truth.*

72. *The ignorant and blind seek Truth only as a solution to their quarrels: however, Truth never appears as a moderator.*

84. *You rejoice on viewing yourself as remembered or desired. A great tribulation results when the eternal Self is glimpsed.*

86. *The world has libraries and colleges for wisdom, but Truth has no dwelling place.*

93. *Do not give that which has beauty and Truth to the masses. They can profane the most holy. Do not give the source of power to the greedy mob, greed will destroy the most powerful.*

96. *Experiencing the Kingdom of Heaven is like the small amount of yeast added to dough. It slowly diffuses and changes the entire nature of the dough.*

102. *The clergy are like a dog sleeping in the hay of a manger. The dog cannot eat the hay, but prevents the hungry cattle from finding nourishment.*

104. *When Truth is manifest, how can one think of sinning or of error? Only when one is in the dark, should one seek purification of the self.*

107. *The Kingdom of Heaven is like the shepherd who left his flock of one hundred to find his largest sheep who had wandered off, and when the sheep was found he told it that it was the most cared for.*

10. The Opposing Forces

The strongest opposition to finding Heaven on earth is the conditioning or training gained from society and the acceptance of a fixed wisdom or teachings that suppress the elements of heaven. The goal of the rulers of a society can be explained as keeping the society stable and functional without conflict of its members with either its rulers or its wisdom. This goal is, however, generally in opposition with the individual goals of evolving or becoming more and more knowledgeable, powerful, and independent.

Nevertheless, a stable society is absolutely essential for maintaining a complex world above that of animals. Society does this by controlling the spoken and written language that includes the teaching and enforcing of a constant wisdom or description of society, the rules and methods of interacting, as well as the overall limits of behavior. Society also has to develop and train its members to step into many different positions or roles in order to keep itself running and efficient.

Society must not teach or support the wisdom and skills that can make individuals independent of society. This can be compared to the parental role in raising children. Parents want their children to be talented and intelligent, but not to become uncontrollable. To keep children in conformance, they are conditioned with religious, moral and political concepts that bind them to the family and society. The majority of parents believe that society and its institutions are greater than any individual, and any individual that desires to reach maturity must learn from the wisdom in the home and the institutions of society.

In the past, however, there was an acceptance that some individuals could find knowledge within themselves and hence could know more than what social institutions deemed to state as truth. This inner understanding was called *knowledge* (or *gnosis* from the Greek) to separate it from socially accepted wisdom. Those who believed in an inner source of knowledge were called *Gnostics* before they were condemned and persecuted by Rome and the early Christian church. Today the concept of inner knowledge is further confused with the merging of meaning between knowledge and wisdom, as well as the usage of the word *agnostic* to mean not believing in a god rather than not accepting an inner source of knowledge.

In order to avoid assigning the creative and manifested brilliance of individuals to their inner personal power source, such individuals are labeled as being filled with the power of genius. Use of the term *genius* to describe productive contributors to society (who may or may not have high IQ scores) carries the modern implication that the individual is not the source of creativity, but rather their creative works are due to some arbitrary Divine gift from above. Therefore, a person who can produce new innovation, ideas, or find righteousness is declared to be filled with the power of genius or the creative power from an external god.

This assignment of the source of creativity or righteousness to the heavens above rather than to an inner power means that any individual seeking to become creative or righteous will be looking in the wrong place for guidance and knowledge. Their efforts, for instance, will be to placate and supplicate the heavens above for the desired knowledge and creative powers, rather than developing the inner source. Others may search for creativity by attending how-to workshops or reading self-improvement books such as this one.

Society in general suppresses true individualism and attempts to replace it with an approved individual nature or identity. Individuals are trained to reflect the family or institutional ideals. It is the development of an institutional value and identity that makes it difficult to attempt to discover the *true you* later in your life. The concept of self-perfection can generally only be based upon the social standards that surround you. As an example, a righteous individual has learned not to claim to possess a source of inner power. To do so would result in being labeled an extreme egotist, but the righteous will rather put on an acceptable humble nature and credit some outside power in order to remain active in society.

Society uses techniques to control their members that are identical with the techniques used to control automatic machines or robots.[50] This is done by setting upper and lower limits on each particular behavior response. For instance, you must be friendly, but not too friendly. You must be respectful, but not subservient. You cannot be conceited, yet you must think well of yourself. You should not speak too loudly nor too softly. You must speak the truth, but not if it is uncomfortable to others. Every physical action must not be done too fast nor too slowly. You should be happy, but not overly joyous nor depressed.

To reinforce the limits set by society, members are also taught to judge the actions of each other. Since others in your society are judging you, then you must judge yourself by the same standards so as not to be guilty of some excessive, minimal or unacceptable behavior. You must become very concerned about what "they" might think. It is this continual judgment of yourself and others that helps to keep individuals in bondage to the laws of society.

Once you judge others, there is a change that takes place within you that results in becoming self-important and places you as the center of your world. The more you judge, the greater your self-importance and egocentricity. Self-importance is commonly evidenced as believing that you have all of the wisdom that is required and that you have also attained everything that is important. This ability to judge is

---

[50] Peck (2001)

developed in early childhood where you assumed the role of responsibility in games or with siblings. As you judge others, you become *self*-righteous and fully step into the role of being perfected. Thinking that you are perfected, you can no longer be open to others, but only see others as you desire them to be. This is, of course, bondage to your conditioned concepts of what things should be.

Because they can accept themselves as perfect (or at least almost so), *self*-righteous individuals are afraid of losing control and losing their superiority over others. They have nothing more to gain, but consider that they have a great deal to lose. Because they falsely believe that they are nearly perfect, their ideas and thoughts must therefore also be nearly perfect. This gives rise to their inability to accept any concept or idea other than their first thought or concept. Their first impressions are therefore their prime connection to the outer world and they have great difficulty in accepting later thoughts or inputs. They fear to step into a new world where an unknown heaven dictates what is right and wrong instead of their own perfected conditioning. It is for this reason that dogmatism is always perceived with the *self*-righteous as they cling tighter and tighter to the tenets of some religion or other institution. This clinging to what is conceived as right leads quickly to the joyless nature so commonly observed with the *self*-righteous individuals.

The social conditioning and its powers can be illustrated in an early childhood interaction, where a girl wearing a new dress and believing that she comes from a superior family has an aversion of playing make-believe with other children who want her to be a beggar-thief groveling in the dirt. To play she must surrender her self-importance and her judgments about rights and wrongs and trust in the imaginary game, but perhaps even more importantly, she must somehow break free of her concern about what her parents might think.

The opposing forces of society can also readily be seen in considering what happens to those experiencing first love. The first observation of the couple is that they have gone crazy without any concern for society or others. They are seen as sinking into their own isolated world that no one else can penetrate or understand. Parents, teachers, friends and relatives have the growing fear that they will lose their relationship with the lovers and that they will forget them and go their own unknown way. Even though each of the lovers may function very well and indeed may be better in their daily tasks or assignments, they are a question or embarrassment to the surrounding members of society.

The opposing forces of society and its conditioning are finally manifested with the inevitable separation of the lovers from each other and the destruction of their mutual ecstasy. One powerful force that is quite simple is to make the couple prove that they love each other by telling them that their love is not real and cannot last.

As you may well have experienced for yourself, as soon as the lovers start to be concerned about proving their continuous love for each other, they quickly lose the characteristics that were so important to their ecstasy. Instead of doing what they feel moved to do or what feels wonderful, they do what will be considered proving of their permanent and socially acceptable relationship. They not only must prove to society that their love is permanent, but they also must start to prove it to each other. They become, in other words, what society defines mature lovers to be. This definition does not include any of the five characteristics of Heaven. As for example:

1. They become separated in proving their union to the world.

2. They avoid any animated or vitalized expressions or actions.

3. They control and judge their expressions and feelings so that they will be above criticism.

4. They are careful to limit their personal expressions of fondness for each other.

5. They accept their old roles of who and what they should be as they attempt to prove their maturity.

As they, in turn, become concerned with keeping and pleasing each other, they fall into the traps of communication that cannot allow true expression of feelings or thoughts. As for instance, how can one lover tell the other that he or she is not pleased if they are both attempting to prove that they love each other? Communication reduces to the standard social technique of saying what you believe is proper and desired rather than what you actually feel and believe, and hence union is lost.

The experience of first love can many times become an obstacle for creating Heaven with others at a later date. When first love ends with bitterness or the sense of loss, future commitments may be lessened in order to avoid a repeat of the pains of separation. This type of sentiment is found with someone who will not have another pet because of the trauma with the death of an earlier pet.

There is one more major obstacle to creating Heaven and that is the conditioned concept of what constitutes perfection. Religions have taught, for instance, that in Heaven, your every desire is instantly satisfied, you would have the perfect body and mind, and others would satisfy your every sensual desire. It is this expectation of immediate gratification and/or perfection that prevents many individuals from fully accepting their immediate world and experiences or to take responsibility for creating their own elements of perfection.

Now that the major oppositions to the attainment of Heaven on earth have been discussed, the obstacles offered to the development of each of the separate elements of Heaven will be given as follows:

Quickening

There is a possible problem with the ability to use quickening to create a new role and world. The major concern is when individuals, whether children or adults, cannot return to the normal world and remain locked into their imaginary worlds. The prevention of becoming lost in your own imagined roles is to have an overriding dedication or the forceful outer control from parents or more evolved individuals.

The forceful outer control can also present a major problem, as for instance, in the case where a child uses quickening to become the perfect child that his or her parents desire. Because the child adds quickening to the improvement or mastery, the child will progress very rapidly. The tendency of parents is then to increase the demand upon the child with additional studies or work. If the added studies or work do not require creativity, then the child loses the quickening and instead becomes dutiful and obedient without the development of the inner creative center.

In addition to the desire of adults to force children to rapidly master the social world, there is also the prevention of quickening with enforced posture, breathing and muscle tension. For instance, children are taught to stand with the tummy and fanny pulled in and to only breathe in the upper capacity of the lungs. In addition, their early potty training taught them to maintain a tight control and tension in the sexual and anal region of the body to prevent any leakage from the disgraceful body. These disciplines diminish the capability of the body to produce the quickening.

Oneness

Oneness is finding a source of direction and knowledge within the immediate moment rather than from remembered rules of society, and hence society suppresses any such shift in control. You have been conditioned that if you do not consciously control your actions and thoughts in accordance with society's rules, you will get into trouble. Similarly, society cannot recognize a mystical or spiritual coupling between individuals or some goal that is better than societal laws; society must condemn even the concept of oneness. Religious institutions are surprisingly more critical of an independent source of knowledge and union than governments. For instance, most religions require belief from their members rather than critique, review or question. This requirement can be explained by the nature of religious institutions that desire to be known as the interface between individual and a higher power. If individuals can find a direct source of guidance and support from a higher power then obviously the value of churches in the spiritual sense is reduced.

Ecstasy

Ecstasy is very obviously suppressed in any organization since an ecstatic individual becomes under an influence that is neither understood nor controllable by an institution. Ecstasy opens the mind, feelings and responses to a mental and physical state that goes beyond any societal control. Few people ever see the fullness of ecstasy since it is seldom stimulated in the marketplace or within institutional walls. Society is aware, however, of the exuberant creative individual who finds a source of knowledge and expression that is beyond the immediate comprehension of those around that individual. Some of these individuals have changed society for the better, but always with some opposition as any creative person quickly discovers. A simple example of the opposition of society to ecstasy is seen in the individual who when asked how he or she feels may respond with something like, "I feel great, my world is perfect and everyone in it is an inspiration!" That individual is quickly shunned. By contrast, the individual who complains, "I feel terrible, my spouse and I had an argument last night, my world is falling apart, and I have just the worst headache!" is quickly consoled and accepted. These examples illustrate how society places a strong limit on the range of expressing pleasure.

Voluptuousness

It is the fear conveyed by the word *voluptuousness* itself that prevents most individuals from seeking it. It is many times treated as a criminal act in the modern society. If someone is accused of fondling a child or of caressing a fellow worker with a wrong intention they may be imprisoned. Since you seldom can prove your intention, many refrain from the sensual touching of anyone, even their own children. A couple who fondle each other in public can be arrested for indecent exposure or conduct. To hold hands with anyone but your spouse or child in public can result in some public censure. Response to beauty is likewise very limited with perhaps a maximum of expression being the quiet production of tears in public theaters or music halls. To touch, or in particular fondle, a statue can certainly get you quickly thrown out of a museum as well as would standing transfixed and drooling before some painting. Christian churches also generally limit any voluptuous expressions or feelings of their members and instead emphasize quiet suffering as being the ideal Christian goal as they laud the martyrs and those who suffer in their giving. The concern of many churches is for the victims of society and not those that are attempting to master society.

Rebirth

Rebirth is, of course, not tolerated as children are taught to become predictable and responsible individuals. The parents make a decision as to what is the proper role of their child and force the child to accept and adhere to that role. Institutions later add to this control by adding further definitions of what it means to be a member of a particular institution, religion, political party etc. You experience the effects of even small variations in your behavior or demeanor with comments from people around you who pointedly will ask, "What happened to you?" or "What's wrong with you?"

The physical manifesting of a role may be different from the inner concept of the self. A child may, for instance, step into the physical role of loving his sister, as demanded by the parents, yet inwardly see her as a threat. Most individuals who attempt to present the reborn aspect of being loving or confident face the inner counter awareness of themselves. This results in what is called hypocrisy that is not a true rebirth and is instead a continuation of the playacting of a child.

In conclusion, the oppositions to entering Heaven on earth can be stated as societal teachings or the sins of our parents. Or as stated in religious terms, the sins of Adam.[51]

---

[51] Peck (1999), Ch.12

11. Prerequisites

The first prerequisite for approaching Heaven on earth is to recognize a power higher than your conscious self. The second prerequisite is to yield or surrender to that higher power and then trust it.

An explanation of these two prerequisites begins with considering a very interesting aspect of causing a change to take place. Any change is preceded by a barrier that prevents the change from happening. This barrier is called a *barrier potential* in science and stabilizes the universe. For instance, all combustible materials would have long spontaneously ignited if there was not a barrier to their being ignited. Similarly, if there were no barrier to reading a book that you wish to read, it would have already been read. The majority of people face the barrier potential quite frequently during the day which is generally first manifested in getting out of bed. The second might be getting out the door to go to work and then, of course, the problem of starting work.

You might, for instance, have tried a few breathing techniques[52] and desire to exhale deeper during the day. You may reason that there should be no trouble in doing this except that you quickly find that there are many problems that constitute a barrier to doing it. You might list the problems such as being concerned with what others might think, or that it might distract you, or

---

[52] Peck (1976), Ch. 3

113

that the change might not last etc. All of these items constitute a barrier potential that keep you from spontaneously changing.

In the vast majority of cases of overcoming a barrier potential, the energy to break through it comes from an external source and many times has a very mystical quality to it. Physicists are very much aware of this in terms of nuclear and quantum reactions, psychologists are aware of this as clients suddenly do change their view of the world, or a parent suddenly finds that Junior no longer resists doing homework. In attempting to determine what prompted the change, a clear cause and effect can seldom be found. Generally, the overcoming of a barrier can be said to have taken place because of the rising of an environment supportive to the change itself.

Many righteous individuals will cite the necessary encouragement they received that allowed them to overcome some barrier that stood in the way of their success. Sometimes all that is required is for someone to say, "Oh, you can do it!" and the barrier disappears. Young boys rely upon their friends many times who dare them to jump into the cold pond or to ask the girl for a date. Girls may tend to follow a heroine or example set by more experienced girls or women as they tell themselves, "If Sally could do it, so can I!"

Behind the paternalistic views of the modern world, there are still many persistent concepts about the power of a "good woman"[53] to effectuate the dissolution of barriers both in her husband as well as in their children. The marketplace likewise considers the availability of a mentor to be invaluable to those wishing to master their world.

In the absence of an external individual who can provide the power to overcome your barriers, it is possible to find the power within yourself as in the above illustration about Sally. Many religions describe this as taking upon yourself the name or power of some powerful person or deity. In the Western world this is sometimes called emulating your hero or heroine, which is an argument for maintaining heroic traditions within a society.

Finding a power within yourself begins in childhood with becoming some other person in play. A child will generally emulate his mother or father and attempt to behave and act like they do. This can then be extended to childhood fantasies where super powers are envisioned. In effect, the child imagines the person being emulated within themselves and then relies upon that person becoming real to direct their thoughts, actions and feelings. The imaginary playmate is perhaps an example of the next step in manifesting the inner power. The child initiates the desire to have a playmate and then allows the desire to become manifested using their inner power to imagine and

---

[53] See *Adhisthana* in Glossary.

create. The resulting playmate is generally a much different person than the child. That created person may have courage when the child is fearful, or wisdom when the child is mentally slow. The created playmate is found to be a powerful addition to the child. Many children require a special technique in addressing their playmate that may remind an observer of some religious rite.

A child in being asked to remember a name as mentioned earlier, might believe that the answer comes from an imaginary playmate or some other character that the child has experienced in play. Unfortunately, many adults forget this process of using an inner higher power as they learn to rely upon memorized data and conditioned responses instead. An adult would be quite offended if someone were to suggest that he take an imaginary playmate with him or talk with an inner created fantasy character in order to find some unknown object to solve a particular problem, to critique some idea, or to present some new concept.

There are a number of mental techniques being sold that essentially duplicate the lost methods of childhood. One general adult method is to search through imagined file cabinets, books, videos, reruns of past scenes etc. for answers to questions or problems. Some religions suggest talking to an imagined god or saint in much the same manner. An even more practical method is to assume that some person you meet or some article you read has some teaching or answers that you require or will require, and you must search through all that is encountered.

As experience and faith in some system is gained, then the process becomes more internalized, such as the example of waiting for the desired name to appear without any effort on your part. Materialists might argue that the process is relying upon some continual subconscious brain process to present the required data, yet the more the inner power is relied upon, the more it finally becomes obvious that a connection far beyond your own memory or mental capability is required.

12. Three Vital Requirements

In order to find a new world, new life or Heaven on earth, three basic requirements must be met. The first is that you must mentally create or have a knowledge of the desired world. The second is that you must be able to relinquish concern and attachments for your present world of existence, and the third is that you must have a body and mind capable of continuously supporting the demands of the created new world.

To enter into the extremely different world of Heaven on earth, an individual must start with some basic feelings and knowledge of each of the five elements of Heaven. With the knowledge of the separate elements, you must then mentally create the Heaven that contains all of the elements functioning together. This new world cannot be learned or gained from someone else since it is so hidden, but rather can only be found through the creative action of the self. This creation cannot take place if you are in any manner limited as to future actions by your past conditioning. In this sense the past world must be renounced as if it does not exist. Since the new world is so creative, stimulating and responsive, the inner power center must be freed from any restraints as well. You must become as a child who is able to step into any new game and role with complete trust and excitement.

You cannot be either a good, rebellious or an independent individual; Heaven will reject each of them. The good person attempts to fully conform to society while the rebellious person becomes more self-centered and self-important. The independent person or "lone wolf" closes his outer world such that his learning becomes very limited and generally is limited only to his particular interests. These paths and their variants through life can be readily seen as preventing the attainment of the knowledge of the elements of Heaven.

You cannot be as a child who has not yet learned and mastered the requirements of your society. The knowledge about the elements of Heaven can only be obtained when you have gone beyond your normally limited conditioned responses and instead, fully meet the challenges or demands of life with your total capabilities. If, however, you are reluctant to face the challenges of life and avoid accepting any challenge that requires extra powers, you will never experience even the short exposures to the heavenly powers.

The second step requiring the relinquishment to your attachments to your present world is a very difficult step. The Buddha made a pointed reference to this when he told some ascetics that they hadn't given up all attachments since they still clung tightly to their begging bowls. Most people are very reluctant to give up anything with only a promise of finding something better. The desire for security dominates much of the actions of the members of a society. Any change in your life that may threaten your feeling of security is strongly resisted. For instance, you may be reluctant to change the style of clothes that you wear because of the possible loss of respect or acceptance. Fear of the unknown is rampant within the modern world. Fear about your health, your appearance, losing loved ones, losing a job or losing your memory dominate the minds of most people. Fear of failure, loss and death are dominant reasons why Heaven and its elements are not found.

This is obvious in facing an emergency that requires a short entry into Heaven to find extra powers. If you have any doubts about being able to meet the need, you will be unable to fully react. This requirement is also well recognized by athletes or those individuals who require the access to a perfect body or mind. Self-doubt or limitations stop the entry into the state of perfection or the *zone* as athletes call it. You encounter this as you remain quiet in a group because of fear that someone might think less of you. The ability to renounce is generally only gained in the mastery of life as faith in the future is gained. This faith is built upon the certainty that you have an inner guiding power that is metaphysical and beyond the control of the outer world.

The third requirement of having a body and mind capable of supporting Heaven becomes more understandable with the mastery of life as you become familiar with the requirements of finding success. Probably every successful person would quickly point to the necessity of having a sufficient physical energy level capable of meeting each crisis and a mental dedication and faith that can withstand doubts, uncertainties and distractions over the long periods of time it takes to reach for and find perfection.

Knowing the elements of Heaven is not sufficient for stepping into Heaven. It is like setting a stage and costumes for a play, but not having a script. It is interesting that many Christians will talk about how beautiful their Heaven after death will be, yet have no concept at all as to what they will do there. There must be a purpose or reason to be in Heaven as well as in life, or else there is only a meaningless existence leading to death. In other words, suppose you know and can experience the five elements of Heaven and are able to relinquish your attachments to your present world and have sufficient creative and sustaining energy. Now what do you do? What do you want to do?

You had to have had a dedication in life that led you to the gates of Heaven, but the question of what you want to do next becomes of paramount importance in stepping into Heaven. If you have no clear purpose or goal in the furtherance of your life, you may well take the energy, creativity and responsiveness that you have gained and apply it so some fantasy or short-term desire that leads nowhere. You may have observed this phenomenon as individuals who have found or approach great success in life, seem suddenly to lose their sense of values and become overcome with temptations and vice.

The problem of deciding what you want to do is not only the most important aspect of entering into Heaven, but it is also the least understood, questioned or experienced. The answer to this question obviously must be founded upon another even more important question and that is what do you desire to do, not only with your total life, but also with your existence even beyond?

There is a remarkable characteristic about looking at your future. It is quite easy to envision future suffering and pain, but nearly impossible to envision improvements in your life. For instance, a person can state that, "Not even in my wildest dreams could I have anticipated my present glorious world." Similarly, a person suffering with a broken bone can state, "It was nowhere near as bad as I thought a broken bone would be." It is this magnified fear of the future and the hope against hope that somehow there can be some happiness or security that keeps many institutions in business, promising some future happiness paid for in some form of up-front cash with no questions asked.

Therefore, when most people are questioned as to what they want from life, the answers tend to be generally vague or they limit their answer to something like wanting to find security and happiness which is, of course, the path toward isolation and death.

For those individuals who answer the question with something like, "Well, I really don't know, but I often think about it," there is hope. This answer implies the conflict between conditioned goals or duty and long-term, deep-seated goals that generally are already providing the direction taken in life. As an example of how this functions, consider that if you were curious as a child and found that your curiosity about the world kept increasing as you matured, it is no doubt also a part of your current world. You might extrapolate this observation into describing a path through life that constantly desires to discover and experience more in life. The conditioned brain has a problem, however, in thinking of death which would be the end of this search, and hence the goal suddenly becomes absolutely meaningless.

If heaven on earth is to become a reality there must be the expectation and faith that there is the continuation and fulfillment of life as you probe ever deeper into its mysteries and ecstasy. Death cannot be the end of this exploration. All of those who find Heaven on earth and describe it, tell of the absence of death and the entering into a continuing and unfolding eternal reality.

When you reach the opening of Heaven on earth, you already know of the metaphysical inner power within yourself that directs you through life and is able to change your world and what you are in order to expedite your search. This search and the power behind that search becomes the true eternal reality and not your physical body and objects in the worlds you pass through. The traveler is identified as the soul who is equally at home in a nightmare or in a love scene, in childhood or in aging, in fear or in trust. You know that you enter one world as easily as you enter another. You know that you have passed through a number of different lives in living this life with the same ease as you step from one dream into another. The reality is not in the dream but in the observer and the process of travelling. You and those in union or oneness with you, direct the path to be taken but cannot choose the steps.

The righteous or superior individuals stress the importance of a positive faith in the future as does the ancient literature. Without it you are indeed dying, but with it you can find life eternal.

13. To Become as a Child

Jesus stated[54] that to enter into the Heaven on earth you must become as a child. Nietzsche[55] writes that becoming as a child is the final metamorphosis in becoming a perfected being. These statements create questions in the mind of modern materialists since almost everyone prides themselves as having put away their childish behavior. Other than perhaps the purity of childhood, adults in general see few characteristics of a child that can be admired, much less adopted. However, even the purity of childhood quickly fades as a positive trait when it is identified with being dependent, gullible or naïve. Who wants to be as a child completely dominated by sin or the conditioning of society and genetics?

It is interesting, therefore, to note that many great people are described as having childlike characteristics. But in general, these traits add to the greatness of the individual and seldom detract from it. The childlike traits can also be overlooked and excused because of the great contributions that the individual may have made to society. Some of the childlike traits that are used in describing the great people are:

1. Unbounded energy,

---

[54] Matthew 18:3-4
[55] Nietzsche (1954), Zarathustra's Speeches, see On the Three Metamorphoses.

2. Absolute trust in their future,

3. The intense and seemingly uncontrolled, projection of their feelings,

4. Unconcern for convention,

5. The ability to change their natures or roles in different situations, and

6. Their openness and receptivity.

These traits can also, of course, be stated as being elements of Heaven and trust.

Seldom are these childlike traits considered to be the source of greatness by the average person, since they had to work so hard to remove those characteristics from their own life. You can imagine the shock, therefore, when Jesus told his audience that they should become as children if they hoped to enter the Kingdom of Heaven.

Children do have characteristics that allow them to grow at a tremendous rate, learn languages within an incredibly short time, master the intricacies of behavior in a modern society, and advance in knowledge and skills far beyond any other animal. Physiologists state that a large part of the explanation for human beings being so superior to other animals is that humans spend a much longer relative period of time in childhood when learning rates are highest.

Perhaps the chief difference between childhood and adulthood noted by Jesus and other sages was that children possess a far greater creative energy or quickening than do adults. It is easy then to see how children could use this quickening to lose themselves in their own created world, approach ecstasy and the enjoyment of their bodies and senses, as well as be able to play different roles. These traits suggest, as noted previously, a few of the attributes associated with Heaven on earth.

In contrast to these childlike traits, society wants children to master conformance to the outer world, attain the ability to assimilate data and facts, master routine and repetitive skills, and find the necessary life skills to procreate and maintain a family. Society, in general, considers that when children become about five years of age, they are ready to start putting away childlike traits and to start learning the characteristics of the adult world.

At this age the child has mastered the essentials of language and the basic fundamentals of conforming to society from his or her parents. Schools are then considered to have the task of continuing to teach basic discipline and obedience to authority and law. This is then followed by learning the data and skills necessary to working and living in a technological society. In this regard, the Japanese schools are the envy of many educators who see how the Japanese use much more discipline in their schools, such as forcing children to bow to their teachers, recite in unison, talk only when spoken to, march quietly from class to class, etc. The modern, highly efficient factories of Japan give strong support to the importance of their disciplined schools and institutions.

In terms of society and its institutions, there are almost no arguments in favor of quickening and its creative powers or the other elements of Heaven. The Japanese factories, for instance, threaten the economies of the less disciplined factories of the West. Ironically, their factories and processes were meticulously copied from the Western systems and then totally re-established within their disciplined work place. Their results certainly present hard evidence of the value of discipline and the tight conformance of individuals. Violence is almost unknown in tightly controlled nations where freedom of individual expression is suppressed. With tight governmental control, religious institutions likewise retain power over individuals and control life even within the homes.

Quickening and its creativity, however, do prove their worth by initiating the advances of society. In tightly controlled societies, new patents or inventions are seldom obtained. For example, Japan lags considerably behind the U.S. and suffers from the lack of new creative solutions to their unique and increasing problems. As quickening is suppressed, innovation and individual growth is likewise suppressed. The very concept of becoming more alive has no meaning in any repressive society.

To return to the teaching that you must become as a child to find Heaven, it can be restated that unless you can find or keep the inner creative quickening force of becoming more or evolving, as does a child, society will limit who and what you are and do.

Similarly, children spend a great deal of their time in the state of oneness being completely absorbed in their world. Children have the ability to become totally engrossed in observing someone or some object or activity.[56] Parents are many times embarrassed when their child looks at some stranger's face with intense rapture and absorption. Children can likewise become overpowered in some role that they wish to play. As an example, consider the case when a child decides to be really good. After making the choice of being good, the child assumes a starting role that might be putting on a sweet smile, but then the child is completely dependent upon being open to the parents or other adults for further directions. This starts with opening to a sensitivity of facial expressions such as smiles and frowns. The reaction is simple: if a smile appears, they increase what they are doing and if a frown appears they reduce their actions. As children perfect this ability to fully play a role, they learn to use other less obvious or subtler types of controls such as perceiving changes in others' body tension, actions or roles.

It is this opening and sensitivity to others that is called *samadhi*[57] in the East and becomes the entrance into

---

[56] See *Dhyana* in Glossary.
[57] See *Samadhi* in Glossary; Peck (1998) Ch. 22

being at oneness with a group of people. As the intensity of *samadhi* increases, a deeper and deeper awareness of others is found that can ultimately lead to a knowledge of their most inner feelings as well as their response to the near future. Many individuals report this awareness within a closely coupled group that anticipates the needs and actions of each other. Children are, however, limited in choosing or anticipating their future and instead remain open to outer or preconceived demands.

Childhood is used as an example of purity. Children accept their world and themselves without regret, blame, excuses, and concern for their future. They yield completely to exterior controls and are capable of sacrificing themselves with great pleasure to someone whom they deem is more powerful or knowledgeable than themselves. During this surrender or sacrificing of themselves, they demonstrate ecstasy whether it is in submitting to having their tummy rubbed or to the power of a wicked witch in one of their imaginary games. Children can be observed to die in a game with an apparent degree of good feeling as they moan, scream and writhe in their imagined death throes and certainly appear to approach ecstasy. Children find some inner feelings that are easily called ecstatic which begin with the complete acceptance of outer forces followed by a rising inner sense of pleasure as they submit and sacrifice themselves to the demands. This surrender causes the increased flow of the inner quickening energy that is extremely pleasurable.

Any adult who has held small children wiggling with pleasure as they are caressed is being given a lesson in the voluptuousness of the bodies of children. Children love contact games and stimulation of their bodies such as with playground slides, teeter-totters or simple running and jumping. Children love cuddling with soft furry toys, rubbing their faces with their blankets and sucking their thumbs. Similarly, children can become fascinated with some piece of plastic, rock or trash that overpowers them and holds them spellbound in a feeling that few adults can find even in the front of some masterpiece of art.

A child is reborn many times a day as new roles are put on in play or in front of different people. A child, for instance, can become a pathetic tragedy as a knee is scraped in front of mommy, yet stoically grin with a much greater wound when playing with a bigger child. Children are so sensitive to playing or experiencing new roles that it is easy for a child to become obsessed with some role for months after viewing some emotional or threatening movie or show. Adults are likewise affected, but they are hardened to return to their own role, whereas a child is not as habituated to a fixed role.

Children can find or experience all of the basic characteristics of Heaven on earth except that they cannot define Heaven nor do they have the inner power to remain in Heaven. Children do not know enough of themselves and the outer world to be able to envision a world much more evolved than what they have. They are busy responding to and exploring their immediate world which is bordered by the unknown. They can see the world of the adult, but it is shrouded in darkness since they do not have the developed skills, sensors and understanding to enter it. They are as closed to the mature world as the Heaven on earth is closed to most adults.

This may be a good place to also discuss the effectiveness of drugs as opening a door to Heaven on earth. Many individuals believe that alcohol and other mind-altering drugs can free them from the constraints of the outer world such that they can attain some of the characteristics of childhood. This is true, and under the influence of alcohol and certain other drugs, people can find the sense of oneness, ecstasy, and voluptuous nature normally long lost since childhood. However, drugs generally leave the individual as a child without the ability to know or control the future. Drug users also generally lose the ability to increase their inner vital energy, and although they can drop or modify their normal role to some degree, they seldom can find a rebirth in a new role and world other than suggested by their immediate surroundings or associates. The ancient spiritual practices that require a discipline of both body and mind offer a far better way of refinding the states of childhood but are beyond the scope of this book.[58]

---

[58] Peck (1998), Ch 22

14. The Many Steps

The path that leads to your Heaven on earth is traveled with many very small steps. However, even a small step may sometimes open a door that will reduce the number of steps and time required for the trip. The steps taken are never planned nor controlled, yet after they are taken, it can be seen that they were all leading toward a constant goal set at the beginning of the trip.

Because an individual's metaphysical or spiritual powers are quite weak, only small changes in your world can be obtained at any one moment. It therefore takes many small steps to reach any intentional long-range goal in life. Because the inner powers that effectuate change are hidden and not consciously controlled, your thinking, judgmental and conditioned mind must find and trust another source to direct each step.

Some researchers in the fields of parapsychology and the paranormal have ceased attempting to find evidence of individuals being able to obtain large and miraculous changes, such as suddenly having the ability to play the piano, or the power to read and speak an unknown foreign language, or to lift a piano with their mind. Instead, researchers have been quietly investigating the evidence that individuals do have the power to effectuate very small changes in their world. Only well-controlled scientific experiments and statistical analysis, however, will demonstrate this very weak power. As an example, work at Princeton University[59] has given excellent evidence that a directed and controlled mind can influence the operation of machines, although only to an extremely small extent.

The changes obtained in this study can be explained by the mind affecting the normal small variations found in machines. Machines have a natural internal variation of functioning called *noise*. For example, a machine will continually vary its speed going slightly faster or then slower. If speed controls are used, then the variation in speed will be lessened, but it will still change continually. These very small naturally occurring variations require very little energy to shift the machine one way or the other and apparently the mind is capable of delivering such a small amount of controlling energy. As an example of how much change the mind can exert, consider that an individual, who has a good ability to affect the operation of a machine, concentrates upon speeding up a clock and keeps at it for twenty-four hours. At the end of the twenty-four hours, the clock could have advanced about one minute (or for one year; six hours) over what would have been expected.

The human body can likewise be considered to have inner noise with very slight variation in its healing and self-destructive processes. Recent work[60] suggests that

---

[59] Jahn and Dunne (1987), Section Two: Man/Machine Margins
[60] Sicher, et al. (1998)

concerted prayer over an extended period of time from a large number of people can slightly increase the rate of healing of certain patients. The results, however, do not demonstrate any instant cures or miraculous changes, but rather an overall improvement in health over a period of time that is slightly greater than that reported in a control group.

There has long been an awareness of the Placebo Effect. If a person is given a pill that contains no medicine, but told that taking the pill will help an illness, a seemingly miraculous cure may result. One would think that the modern pharmaceutical companies would be embarrassed with their test results of some new drug when it is compared with a sugar pill or placebo. Pharmaceutical companies must publish the comparison of their new drug with a placebo and invariably the placebo works quite well for some individuals and when averaged over a number of individuals it still works but not quite as well as the drug. It is as if the body can respond to small inner variations, or noise, that produce a small step toward obtaining the desired change in symptoms if it is so directed.

Almost everyone is convinced of the power of the mind to make an illness worse. The medical profession is also well aware of how psychosomatic illnesses are many times the sole product of the mind. Similarly, many individuals find that if they have a particular mindset, they can avoid catching some contagious disease that is prevalent around them. There is a technique of diminishing the symptoms of an illness by first using the mind to make the symptoms worse. This is generally fairly easy to do and can be convincing to the conscious thought process that the illness can be affected by the mind. The next step is to minimize the symptoms, which can be assisted in some cases, by imagining the taking of some magic elixir or pill. The interesting result of working with your own symptoms is that you can discover the effectiveness of your own mind in controlling illness.

Another set of experiments studied the ability of one mind to influence another's mind without any contact, in the same manner as changing a machine.[61] The experiments established that if one person concentrates upon a scene containing a geometric form, then another person can find a feeling of correspondence when a similar shape appears in his or her mind. The similar shape then is able to activate the conscious mind much in the same way as the name to be remembered appears to the conscious mind[62] when internal agreement is found.

The inner generation of shapes compared with that within the mind of the other person can be explained as mental noise that creates one image or shape after another. This noise also includes such things as different motions, colors and spatial arrangements.

---

[61] Jahn and Dunne (1987), Section Three: Precognitive Remote Perception
[62] See discussion on p. 22.

This noise can be viewed if you close your eyes tightly and then observe what the eyes are seeing. This noise can continuously produce one shape after another until one matches the shape concentrated upon by the other person. When the two are similar then the mind senses a correlation, similar again to the recognition of a remembered name, and then lets the image become part of the conscious mind.

This process takes time and patience since it may take time for one brain to generate the same shape as that already concentrated upon by another mind. The awareness of a geometric shape is also only the barest of any transmitted intelligence, but over time it can become significant if other shapes can also be added to reinforce a more detailed total image. More information than shapes can obviously be transmitted from one person to another as for instance, when individuals have a common dedication and are actively discussing something of mutual interest. During such times you have probably experienced the other person's concepts, feelings as well as intention that you may describe as knowing what the other person was going to say, or that you knew where the other person was coming from.

The important consideration in the above discussions is that the human mind is capable of exerting a small force that can slightly affect subtle controls within its own physical body and mind. The mind is also able to effectuate small changes in the images, thought, and subtle controls within other individuals, probably similar to its capability to materially change the operation of mechanical machines. This power of the mind to control other disconnected systems is very weak at best, but most importantly if it can maintain that small force over a long period of time it can ultimately accomplish apparent miracles with a step-by-step sequence of events.

In describing this quickened power of the mind, one might consider the mind to have a special subconscious operation that compares the normal variations of the brain and body to a remembered desired result. For instance, the body can be considered to have a constant working comparator[63] that can compare variations of the body and mind with a dedicated goal. If the brain produces a rising thought, image or sound that is related to something that is desired, then the comparator initiates a response such that the body and mind can utilize the change as a small step. As an example, consider the operation of the mind as you wait for the brain to produce the name that goes with a particular face.[64] The comparator watches the noise generated by the brain and when a sound appears that is a part of the name and compares favorably with the remembered face or attribute, the name is thrust forward to the conscious brain.

---

[63] Peck (2001), Ch. 7
[64] See discussion on p. 32.

The model of the comparator can also be used to explain how dedicated individuals are able to see or hear things that assist them in reaching their goals. You have had the experience of talking to someone and then becoming aware of how little they heard of what you said or the reverse when you discover that you missed a great deal of what someone else has said. However, if someone says something that you have essentially instructed your comparator to hear, then, for instance, you can hear the faintest of compliments. The common expression, which is quite true, is that you only hear or see what you want to hear or see. Similarly, if you are dedicated to finding or seeking something new, then you can see and hear things that serve as keys to opening doors to new understandings that no one would have heard or seen if they had not been so dedicated.

To summarize the chapter so far, you have inner powers that can be used to intentionally change your self and world at any instant, but only to a very small degree. However, if the intention or dedication can be maintained over a long period of time then large changes can be obtained. If you are capable of maintaining a constant dedication to what you seek, then you will find that anything related to your goal can be seen or heard. This new idea can then function as a key to further unlock unknown doors that you could not have entered before.

The next obvious question that needs to be addressed concerns setting and maintaining a dedicated path through life toward creating and finding your own

Heaven on earth. The chief question is how can you consciously instruct your inner self or subconscious as to where you desire to go and what you wish to find. As you have already learned, the harder you try to control the subtle natures, the worse things get. How can you bypass your own conditioned thoughts, desires and fears?

This answer can be found in early Indian descriptions of some processes that could bypass the conscious brain and "go straight to the goal." The Sanskrit term for this was *sadhana* which is a common term in the East that is generally now related to religious observances. (Compare *sadhana* with the Greek word *hamartano* or sin, which means "to miss the mark.") *Sadhanas* are practices that an individual can consciously do with applied effort that somehow lead to the subconscious or inner power sources.

As an example, this book discussed how someone might find a sense of voluptuousness in listening to Mozart. In this case, the listening to the music becomes a *sadhana* and the resulting sense of voluptuousness is the result of the *sadhana* and not of some power of Mozart. Similarly, finding peace and beauty in watching a sunset is not due to the sunset or in the looking, but rather the *sadhana* of using the complex interaction of concentration, sunset, vision and expectation and allowing it to magically change your mood.

Meditation was originally a *sadhana* that required an individual to mentally find and then concentrate on the inner sound or *nadam* of the body, now called tinnitus or ringing in the ear. The *nadam* increases with an increase in the energy demand by the inner processes of the body and, as an example, is commonly heard in illness as the inner processes of the body gear up to fight the illness. Normally this inner sound is not heard, particularly amid the clamor of the conscious brain. If the sound can be found, the individual has bypassed the thinking brain and gone directly to listening to the sound of the inner power (or as some religions believe, the sound of the cosmos or *AUM*.)[65] As this source is allowed to dominate the searching brain, thoughts disappear and you are in a sense connecting into the power or energy center of your body, mind and world. If you are able to hear this sound of quickening, then you can learn how to increase or decrease it using the breath, tensions posture, etc.

Similarly, the power of words and descriptions must be understood if they are to be changed or used to describe a goal or the Heaven that you seek. The important consideration about words is that words have been assigned to things and are separate from the things. Changing the name of something does not change the thing but certainly can change the reaction to the thing. This book, for instance, has attempted to assign a different meaning to the word *love* and a different

---

[65] or *OM*

143

meaning to the word *voluptuous* that results in much different responses to the two words as well as to that which they refer. Academicians, politicians and religious leaders have long shifted the meaning of words in order to support their particular purposes. You have no doubt experienced the change in certain words in your own life and find, for instance, that some words are now vulgar or have the opposite meaning to the original usage. You may also have noticed the resulting change in your responses to the things referred to, such as the words voluptuous and love. Words are the basis for much of your conditioning.

As a starting illustration of your very ingrained response to words and their meanings, consider your uncontrolled and unconscious response to the printed word, and attempt to look at a sign without reading or responding to the printed words. You can no longer look at letters as geometric shapes as you did before you learned to read, you can only see and experience words and the meanings that you were impressed with.

As a child, you learned to read by first being told to concentrate upon letters as symbols and that each letter had characteristics that you had to impose upon it. Each letter was imprinted with characteristics that had little to do with the shape of the letter. As a child you looked at the letter "A" and would repeat the name and sound associated with that letter and later could point to words that began with "A." Finally, you had to assign particular meanings to words so that as you looked at a word you experienced the meaning of the word that had nothing to do with the shape of the letters. If a printed word was held up in front of you, you were tested to see if you had attributed the proper meaning to that word and could audibly state the words.

Gradually over time, printed words took on an existence and reality of their own that you cannot now ignore or overlook. Similarly, you assigned a meaning to a person who wore a policeman's uniform or a cleric dressed in religious garb and even now, you probably still react to the uniform and garb as if it has a power of its own. Much of your childhood life consisted of identifying objects[66] and giving them a name and characteristic[67] that would determine how you would react to them later.

This process of giving a name to what you desire is called bringing the sun (the name) and the moon (the object being described) together. This process of assigning characteristics to objects, processes or interactions is called *dharana* in Sanskrit and was considered a beginning *sadhana* in mastering the mental control of life. The objects and interactions in your world can only be perceived if you have a name for them. Most of the names in your vocabulary are, of course, given to you during your education and serve you very well in interacting with the social world. However, in creating your own Heaven on earth, many

---

[66] Form or *rupa* (Skt.)
[67] Name or *nama* (Skt.)

words must be separated from the objects they describe and a new name assigned.

There is a *sadhana* widely used in the world to separate name from form or object called *dhyana* or meditation. This *sadhana* attempts to undo the effects of *dharana* or to clear the brain of conditioned characteristics assigned to an object or person and to perceive things or people as they actually are. *Dhyana* is not generally understood in the modern world nor, for that matter, the difference between form and name. If you are to create a new world it seems obvious that you must first separate name from form of certain experiences, feelings, actions etc., or the sun from the moon[68] as the ancients described it. For instance, to change your world such that you lose weight, the name of food must be changed. Food must become necessary for energy rather than being a symbol of satisfaction and importance. In order to change your feelings about employment, work must become opportunity, challenge, or experience rather than drudgery. As an example of name and form consider the *work* and *play* of children. You are well aware of how children will complain about work that may require far less physical effort than their play.

This ability to separate sun from moon or name from form is commonly acquired while mastering society when doubts arise and individuals seek to find the

---

[68] Peck (1998), Ch. 13

underlying characteristics of objects and people. This is generally related to acquiring the wisdom of seeing the world and individuals as they are. Those with this wisdom state that they have to empty their minds of expectations as they meet someone and must look for a knowledge or *gnosis* that rises up from an inner power center rather than using learned judgment based upon the conduct, dress and speech of others. This process is true *dhyana* or meditation. Similarly, a wise person can read a religious document and look beyond the conditioned meaning of the words and phrases and find a message that is only there for those who have that capability to fully see and hear.

When interacting in oneness with others, it is possible to respond to the needs of the moment without relying upon normal socially conditioned responses. This is called *samadhi* in Sanskrit. This ability is commonly seen when children play together or when adults work collectively toward a mutual demanding goal that requires the full output from everyone.

In *samadhi*, the game or the goal controls the individuals rather than the normal continual judgments as to social acceptability. Generally, most individuals who have entered into this relationship state that they lost their concerns for what they did and rather trusted the group or goal. In such cases, there is, in effect, a controlling hand or guidance that directs everyone so that everyone knows what is being done as well as what will be done. It is as if the group is following some subconscious control or direction. There is also an ancient Sanskrit word for this common direction within a group called *samyama*[69] that means everyone functioning under a common direction or power.

The final necessary requirement for creating heaven is in seeking a heaven. In finding the heaven there must still be seeking to constantly increase the power of heaven. If you do not have a firm dedication to find and expand your created heaven, it will not exist. The process of finding or creating your own Heaven on earth, therefore, consists of many steps, many of which can only be taken with a different view of the mind and the world. The concept of the self as controlling each moment must be given up and rather the goals in life must be allowed to control each step. The teachings of religions of setting a goal in life, trusting in a higher power and then finding ecstasy in all that you do are as true today as they were in millennia past.

In conclusion, a portion[70] of the *Sermon on the Mount*, common to the Western world, can be paraphrased as teaching the way to Heaven:

- *To create your own Heaven, you must always be aware of the inner power that resides in your lower heart and have faith in its ability to transform your life.*

---

[69] See *Samyama* in Glossary.
[70] Paraphrased from Matthew 6:9-13

- *You will learn that the inner power changes you and your entire world and leads you into finding the perfection of every moment in your life.*

- *This power reflects your inner world, which must be kept pure.*

- *The greatest gift is that this glorious power can be fully present in the moment and with you forever.*

Glossary of Important Terms

The respelling of Sanskrit terms is with the Harvard/Kyoto convention, if different.

Adhisthana (adhisSThAna) (Sanskrit)

*From **adhi**: above, **STha**: to stand.*

To stand above. "The power behind the throne."

Agapao (Greek)

*From the root **agan**: very much, **agamai**: to wonder at or to admire.*

The experiencing of love that is overpowering and consuming.

Statements of Jesus further assist in defining *agapao* when he compares himself to a shepherd who would lay down his life for his sheep,[71] and then later tells his followers to love each other as he loves them and then adds that there is no love higher than laying down your life for your friends.[72]

The Greek word, tithemi, behind the translated lay down, is better translated as lay forth, since it does not mean to lay down in dying as commonly rendered, but rather means to place, put, set or commit. A shepherd therefore gives his full

---

[71] John 10
[72] John 15:13

attention to his flock and becomes an example of fully living for his flock or of *agapao*. Jesus also points out that if you *lay your life down* (*forth*), you may then take it again.[73] This can be compared with his statement that whoever loses his life will find it.[74] To *lose your life* also implies the taking up of a new life or of being reborn to fit a new role in life.

Astonied

To be stunned, to grow numb, to be overpowered.

Astonied has been replaced with the word *astonished* that has lost much of the original meaning of being overpowered. The Old Testament used astonied to precede a revelation or insight. For instance, the book of Daniel 4:19 tells of Daniel being astonied for one hour before interpreting the King's dream.

Brahmacharya (*brahmacarya*) (*Sanskrit*)

*From **brahma**: the Divine power; **carya**: the path of.*

Following inner guidance.

Dharana[75] (*dhAraNa*) (*Sanskrit*)

---

[73] John 10:17
[74] Mark 8:35
[75] Peck (1994), Practices; Peck, (1976) Ch. 6

Holding, single pointed concentration.

Dharana is taught in grade schools as children learn to concentrate upon only one thing and then to project some concept upon it. As for example, looking at a word and letting it stand for some particular meaning.

Looking for or projecting a particular attribute onto the object of concentration such as seeing anger in a friend that did not exist before your concentration. Staring or concentrating on a candle and seeing it as alive or as a projection of yourself.

Dhyana[76] (*dhyAna*) (*Sanskrit*)

To meditate, contemplating or observing without judgment.

Similar to *dharana* except that a concept is obtained from the object being concentrated upon. The object of concentration is seen standing completely in its own light.

Observing a friend without preconceived notions and seeing or becoming what they are actually feeling without your bias.

---

[76] Peck (1994), Practices; Peck, (1976) Ch. 7

To meditate upon an object and perceive a usage of it that was not there before. To meditate on your lower heart and finding a power that was unknown before.

Heart

*See the Sanskrit root **hrit** (**hRd**): **hRdaya** (**hRdaya**): heart.*

The center or core, the center of being, feeling and reacting, the lower abdomen, the seat or dwelling place of the source of passion, knowledge, inspiration and strength.

The early Hebrew word for heart, *labab*, also meant to be enclosed by, such as, the heart enclosed the source of quickening. Compare with Cardiac: *Cor* (Latin) from *Kardia* (Greek), which had the early meaning of an inner organ with two orifices such as the stomach or beating heart.

Heaven

*From the root **kamer**: a vault.*

That which rises upwards or exists above; a source of power. A world of perfection or of the perfected (righteous).

Heaven can be your inner lower secret vault or closet (see *tameion*). St. John of the Cross gives a good discourse on the innermost cellar where perfect love is found.

Heavenly

That which is rising or rearing upward. A reflection of that which is above.

Isvara pranidhana (Izvara praNidhAna) (Sanskrit)

Izvara: ruling God; praNidhAna: respectful attention.

Aware of inner guidance.

Madya

From mad: to rejoice, be glad, exult, delight or revel in.

Ecstatic, exhilarating, intoxicating.

Maithuna

Oneness, union, coupled.

Mansa (mAMsa) (Sanskrit)

Flesh, voluptuous, sensual.

Matsya

Quickening, fish, Pisces, vibrant.

Mudra (mudrA) (Sanskrit)

Identifying role, sign, posture.

Nirvana (nirvAna) (Sanskrit)

From nir: out and vA: to blow.

To be blown out, as a candle.

Pancamakara (paJcamakAra) (Sanskrit)

Madya, Matsya, Maithuna, Mansa (mAMsa), Mudra (mudrA).

Quicken

> ***Zoopoieo*** *(Greek) to make alive or more alive; compare with **soma**, **chi**, **ki**, **kundalini**, holy spirit.*[77]

Righteous

> See **dikaios** *(Greek).*

> *To be perfected, made right, balanced, just.*

> *Compare with enlightened or superior individuals, self-directed.*

Sadhana (sAdhana) (Sanskrit)

> *From **sAdh**: to go straight to the goal.*

> *Practices that overcome conditioning.*

Samyama (saMyama) (Sanskrit)

> *From **saM**: together; **yama**: to control: under one control.*[78]

> *To be of one mind with others, free from socially conditioned thoughts and behaviors.*

Svadhyana (svadhyAna) (Sanskrit)

> *From **sva**: the soul, self-identity; **dhyAna**: meditation, attention.*

---

[77] Peck (1985), II Elaboration on the Basics, Vitality
[78] Peck (1994), II. Slokas with commentaries C, Practices

Aware of inner forces.

Tameion (Greek)

> *Storehouse, treasury, lower or hidden store room, heart, inner heaven, or place of the inner power or quickening.*

Tantra (Sanskrit)

> *From **tan**: to manifest and **tanu**: power within the self. **tra**: the means for.*
>
> *The means of bringing forth the inner power.*[79]

Tapas (Sanskrit)

> *Fervor, heat.*

Vajra (Sanskrit)

> *Thunderbolt, the voice of **Indra**.*

Voluptuous

> *Feeling strong visual and tactile delight.*

---

[79] Peck (1998), Ch.9

References

Besant, A. & Das, B. The Bhagavad-gita. (1987) Delhi, India: Anmol Publications (Devanagari plus English)

Goble, F.G. (1970) The third force. New York, NY: Grossman

Jahn, R. G. & Dunne, B. (1987) *Margins of reality*. San Diego, CA: Harcourt Brace.

Lu K'uan Yu (Trans.) (1973) *Taoist yoga: Alchemy & immortality*. York Beach, ME: Weiser

Maslow, A.H. (1954) *Motivation and personality*. New York, NY: Harper and Row

_____ (1993) *The farther reaches of human nature*. New York, NY: Arcana

_____ (1968) *Toward a psychology of being*. New York, NY: Van Nostrand Reinhold Co.

Moody, R. (1975) *Life after life*. New York, NY: Bantam Books

Nietzsche, F. (1984) Human all too human. (M. Faber & S. Lehmann, Trans.) Lincoln, NE: Univ. of Nebraska Press (Work originally published 1878)

Nietzsche, F. (1954) *Thus spoke Zarathustra.* (W. Kaufmann, Trans.) New York, NY: Penguin Books (Work originally published 1891)

Peck, R. (1976) *American meditation and beginning yoga.* Windham Center, CT: Personal Development Center.

_____ (1985) *Handbook for goats.* Windham Center, CT: Personal Development Center

_____ (1998) *The golden triangle.* Lebanon, CT: Personal Development Center

_____ (1988) *The stone of the philosophers.* Windham Center, CT: Personal Development Center

_____ (1994) *The philosophy of Patanjali.* Windham Center, CT: Personal Development Center

_____ (1999) *Power for change.* Lebanon, CT: Personal Development Center

_____ (2001) *Finding power.* Lebanon, CT: Personal Development Center

Patanjali. (1983) *Yoga sutras of Patanjali.* (J. J. Ballantyne & G. Shastri, Trans.). Delhi, India: Parimal Publications (Devanagari with English)

Robinson, J. (Ed.) (1988) The Nag Hammadi library in English. San Francisco, CA: Harper & Row

Abhinavagupta. (1988) *Paratrishika vivarana.* (J. Singh, Trans.) Motilal, India: Banarsidass (Devanagari plus English)

St. John of the Cross. (1959) *Dark Night of the Soul.* (E.A. Peers, Trans.) Garden City, NY: Image Books

St. John of the Cross. (1961) *Spiritual Canticles.* (E.A. Peers, Trans. Garden City, NY: Image Books (Original work published in 16th century CE)

Svatmarama. (1972) *Hathapradipika* (2nd edition). Madras, India: Adyar (Original work published ca. 1350-1550 CE) (Devanagari plus English)

Sicher, F., Targ, E., Moore, D., 2nd, & Smith, H. S. (1998). A randomized double-blind study of the effect of distant healing in a population with advanced AIDS. Report of a small-scale study. *The Western journal of medicine*, *169*(6), 356–363.

Woodroffe, J. (1974) *The serpent power.* Madras, India: Ganesh & Co.

Further Useful References

Liddell, H.G. & Scott, R. (1996) *A Greek-English lexicon: Abridged from Liddell & Scott's Greek-English lexicon*. Oxford, England: Clarendon Press (Original work published 1891).

Monier-Williams, M. (1990) *A Sanskrit-English dictionary*. Oxford, England: Clarendon Press. (Original work published 1899).

Marshall, A. (1975) *The interlinear KJV-NIV*. Grand Rapids, MI: Zondervan.

The holy bible: Authorized King James version. (1970). Nashville, TN: Thomas Nelson (Original work published 1611)

Patanjali. (1983) *Yoga sutras of Patanjali*. (J. J. Ballantyne & G. Shastri, Trans.). Delhi, India: Parimal Publications (Original work published c. 400 CE). (Devanagari with English)

Index

About the Author, the Book, and Contributors

Robert L. Peck is a research scientist with many patents and published papers primarily in the field of energy conversion devices and plastic materials that have similar properties to biological membranes. In order to expedite his work, he formed several corporations with support obtained from the government and large private institutions.

He is married, raised eight children, served as a scoutmaster for twelve years, and is now serving as Director for the Personal Development Center where he teaches, counsels and is engaged in psychological/physiological research.

Bob had mystical experiences as a child, and as a child was unafraid to pursue them to such a degree that he retained many of them into adulthood. He served in the Army as a paramedic in the Pacific near the end of World War II and by several chance meetings was introduced into some of the Eastern practices.

Bob started teaching meditation in industry in the early Seventies at no charge for those who could not afford to pay for Transcendental Meditation. His Westernized meditation became in demand in local churches, adult education classes, and other informal groups. Many of the students, after mastering meditation, desired to experience more of the strange sensations that they were finding within themselves and agreed to enter into experimental groups that would look deeply into the various religious and developmental practices from the East. Everyone agreed to try the practices and report the results without any money exchanging hands in order to keep everyone free from any sense of obligation. These middle-aged and middle-class Americans proved to be very adept at mastering many of the old and diversified Eastern spiritual practices.

As some spiritual scholars and teachers learned of the success of these American groups, they offered support which included books and documents on ancient writings and encouragement to read them as technical and scientific discourses in their original languages. Since Bob had already had experience in translating foreign technical journals, he found that translating ancient Sanskrit writings became relatively easy. Technical writings must define terms and their usage and must provide evidence or means of proving the offered new concepts. This places such writings independent of prior religious or social dogma, but with the requirement that the reader be able to reproduce the described results in their own laboratory, body, mind or group.

Bob found his groups of volunteers ready and willing to attempt to reproduce the early discoveries. During this exciting and revealing period of exploration, he wrote several books to document the findings of the students and to provide a starting basis for new students or experimenters.

Creating Heaven on Earth is the result of the next step of looking at the Jewish/Christian writings in the same manner as was used in studying the Eastern writings. Instead of starting with the Bible, of which Bob still retained much bias from his social conditioning, he focused upon the library found at Nag Hammadi. The *Gospel of Thomas* was recognized as a particularly rich source of data since it indicated a strong connection to the writings of the East. This then led into delving deeper into the New Testament of the Bible using the definitions of terms derived from the earlier Sanskrit translations. This required reverting back to the original Greek writings where complete agreement was found with the literal Greek. This book describes much of this later effort in detail and its surprising results.

At the present Bob lives on a hill deep in the woods of Connecticut in the warm embrace of a small community.